FACES BY FRANÇOIS AND JEAN ROBERT

CHRONICLE BOOKS
SAN FRANCISCO

Library of Congress Cataloging-in-Publication Data:
Robert, François 1946–
          Faces / by François and Jean Robert.
          p.   cm.
          ISBN 0-8118-2793-3
          1. Still-life photography. 2. Face in art. I. Robert, Jean 1945– II. Title
          TR656.5 R63 2000
          779'.092—dc21   99-054704

Design by GITTINGS DESIGN, Chicago and Tucson
Design Consultants, Dana Arnett and Jean Robert
Printed in Singapore

Distributed in Canada by
Raincoast Books
8680 Cambie Street
Vancouver, B.C. V6P 6M9

10 9 8 7 6 5 4 3 2 1

Chronicle Books
85 Second Street
San Francisco, CA 94105

www.chroniclebooks.com

VERY SPECIAL THANKS TO Jim Warych, Jane Gittings, Jean Robert, and Dana Arnett. Thanks also to: Ron Gordon, Gregory Cooper, Tom and Janis McCormick, Pat and Tim Rodeghier, John Boehm, Diane Schmitt, Richard Pels, David Harner, Job Rompa, Natalia Osiatynska, Robin Richman, Jesse Hickman, Floyd Gompf, Bill Goddu, Aggie and Bill Cipolla, José Tapia, Joe Quintana, Lars Topelmann, Richard Gorman, Kim Benge, Stephanie Averill-Arnett, Lars Müller, Kati Robert-Durrer, Leigh Anna Mendenhall, Martin Thaler, Bruce Bever, Betty Barquin, Raymond Gordon, and Michael McGinn.

"What is true of the verbal languages, is also true of the visual 'languages': we match the data from the flux of the visual experience with image-clichés, with stereotypes of one kind or another, according to the way we have been taught to see." — Gyorgy Kepes

INTRODUCTION I have walked many roads and wooded paths with François Robert. I came to know him first as a collaborator, and soon thereafter as both a friend and fellow observer of life. After all these years, what strikes me most about him isn't his ability to shoot great pictures, but rather his unrelenting quest for discovery and documentation. He is a wayfarer and a technician, intensely focused—with mind and camera—on taking full advantage of each and every visual instance worthy of examination.

In the early 1970s, François and his brother, Jean, set out to record and compile a series of photographs simply entitled "Faces," to share with the world their gift of seeing. In the years that followed, to the delight of both artists, this series became a regular topic of conversation when viewed by friends and admirers. Today, François continues this quest for discovery by adding dozens of new faces to this growing portfolio each year. And each new addition never ceases to capture the hidden elements of surprise, discovery, and humor—and the wonderful feeling of affirmation, "Aha! Yes, I see it!" "Look! I love it!"

A pair of pliers becomes a bird, a piece of driftwood becomes a whale, and a paintbrush becomes a spiky-haired youth. Dare we call these magical photographs visual puns? François would argue that these creatures are just as alive in their ability to fascinate as they are in communicating a sense of human character. Making this connection for yourself will confirm his notion that these candid expressions offer life to the lifeless, and a sense of soul to our often inane surroundings. — DANA ARNETT, CHICAGO, ILLINOIS

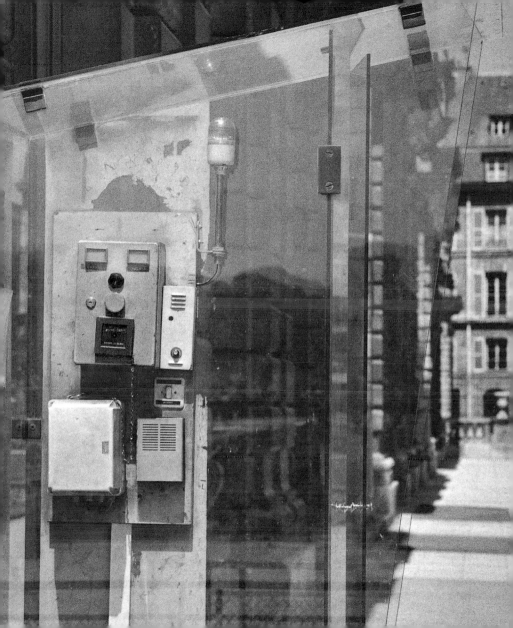

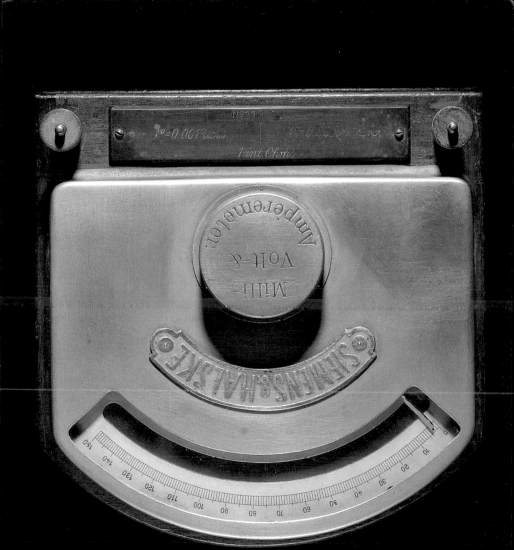

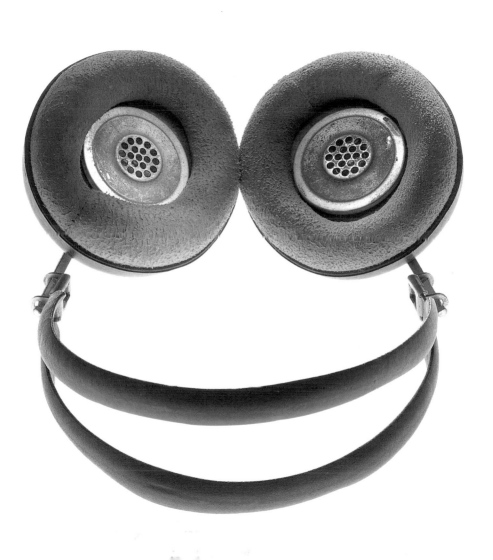

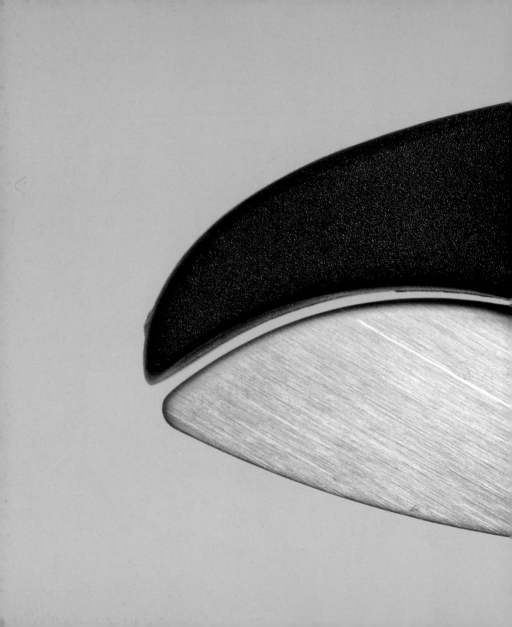

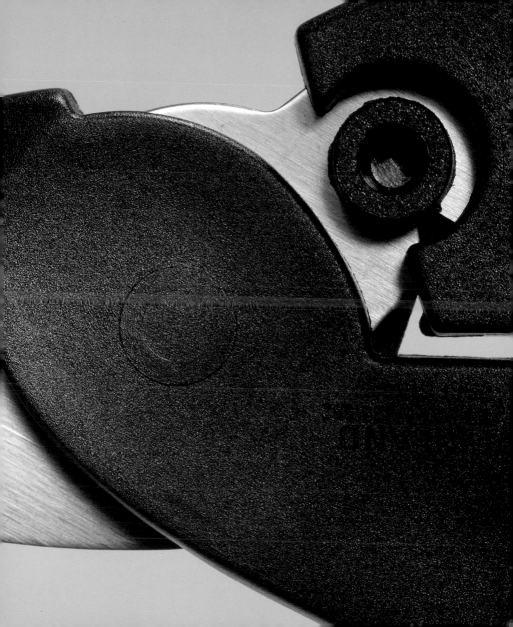

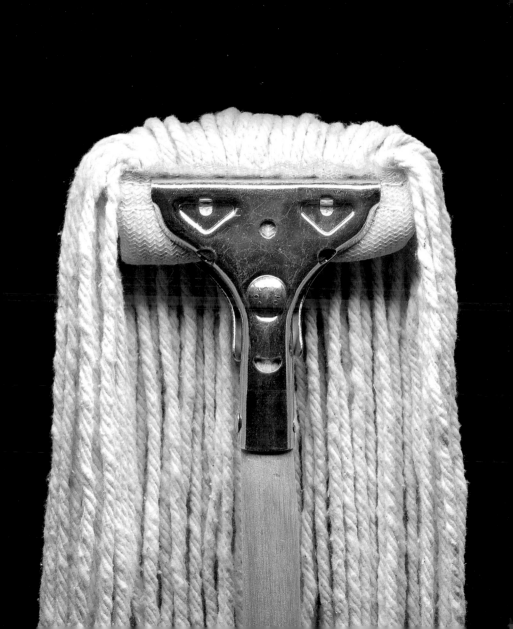

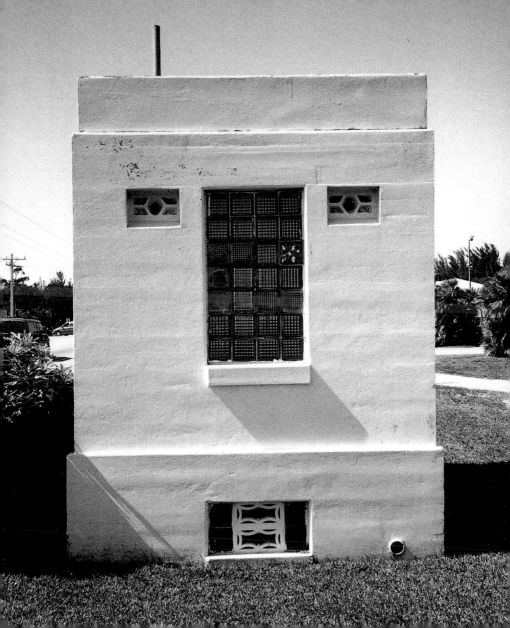

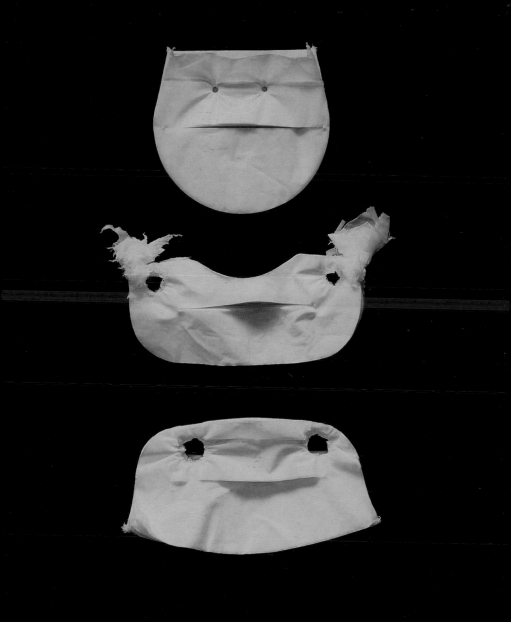

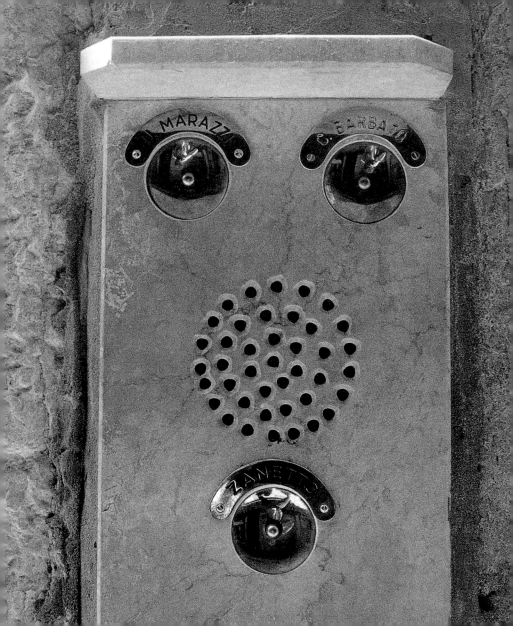

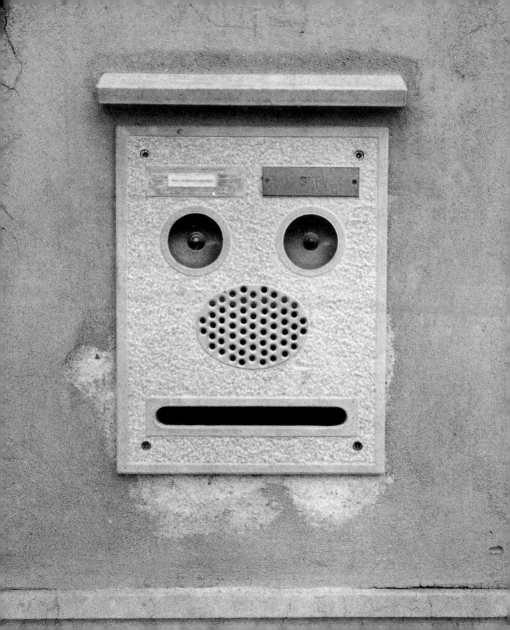

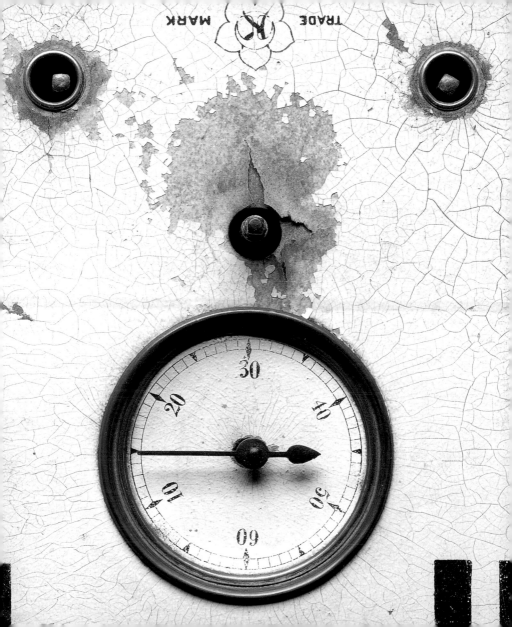

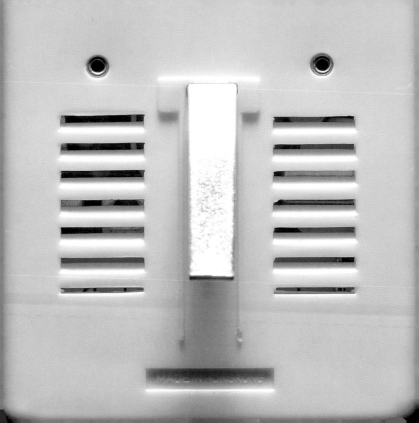

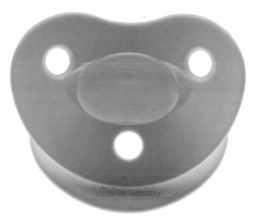

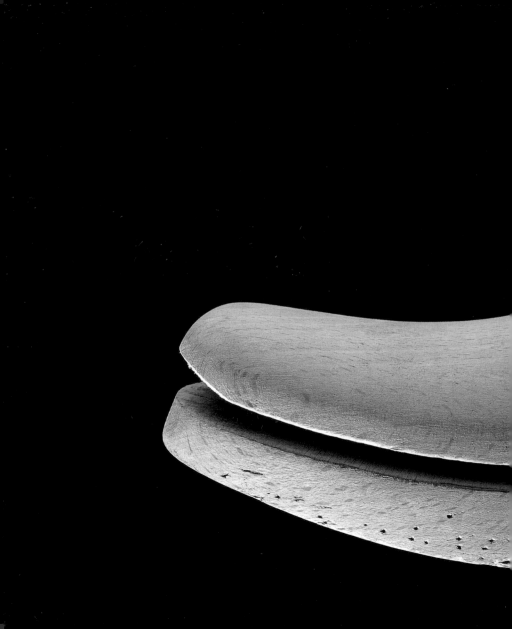

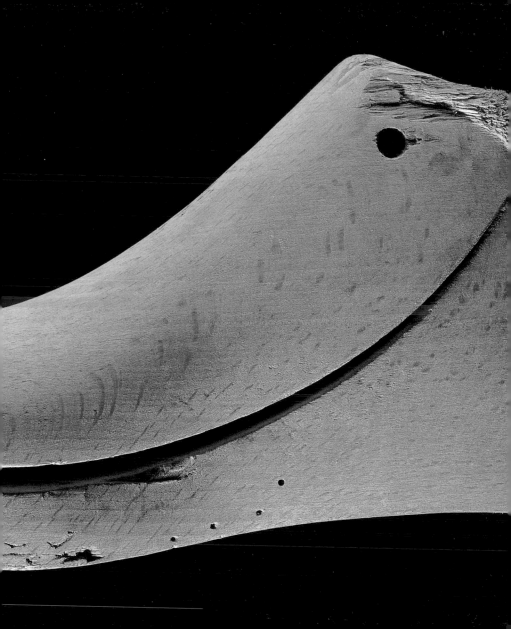

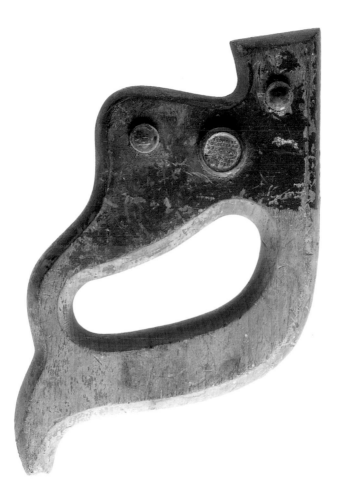

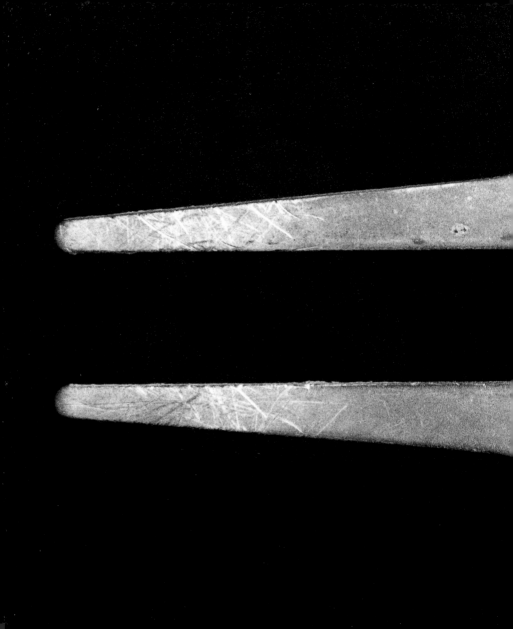

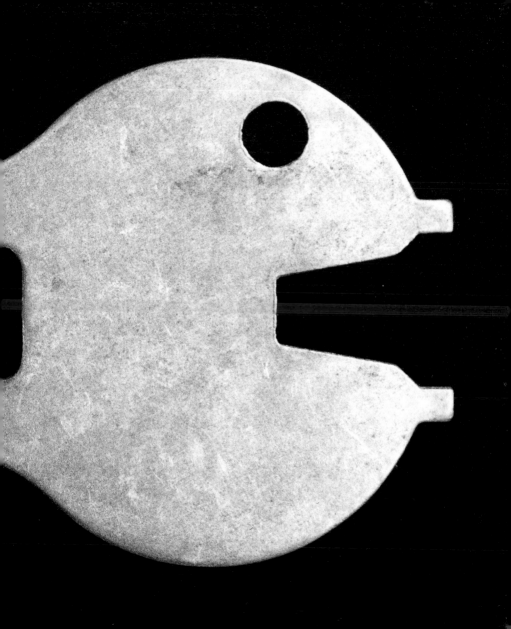

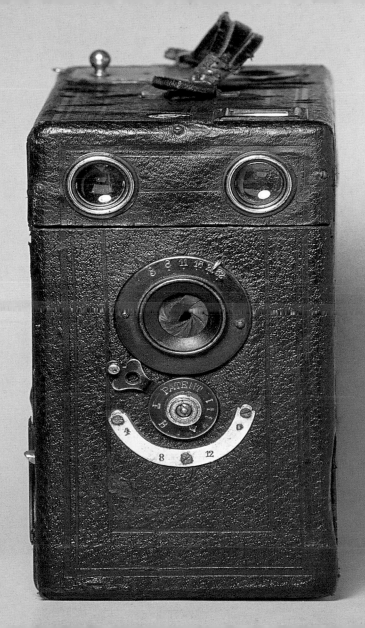

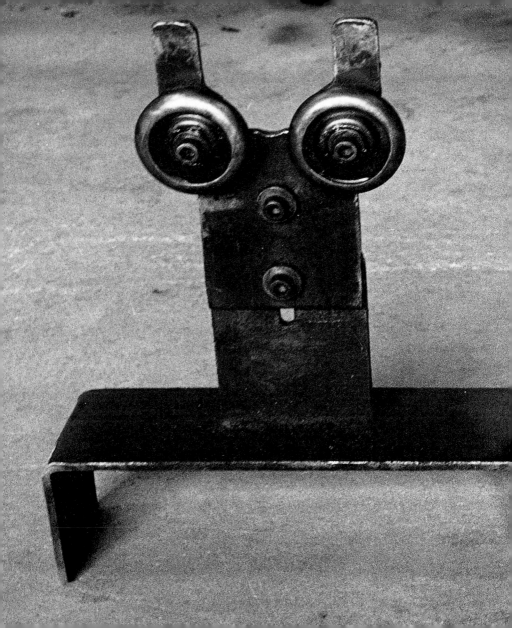

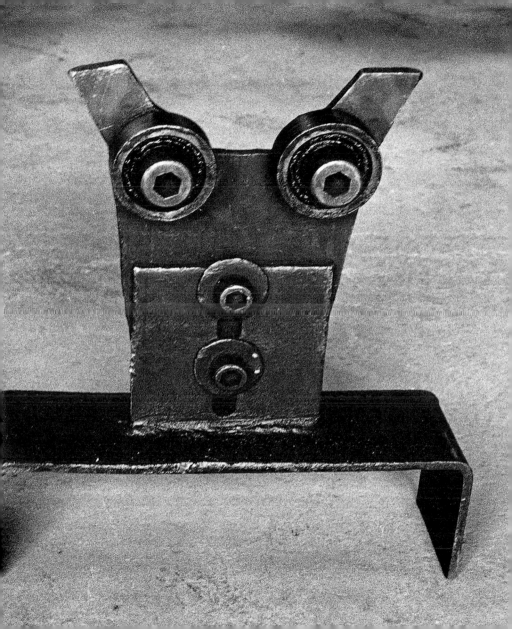

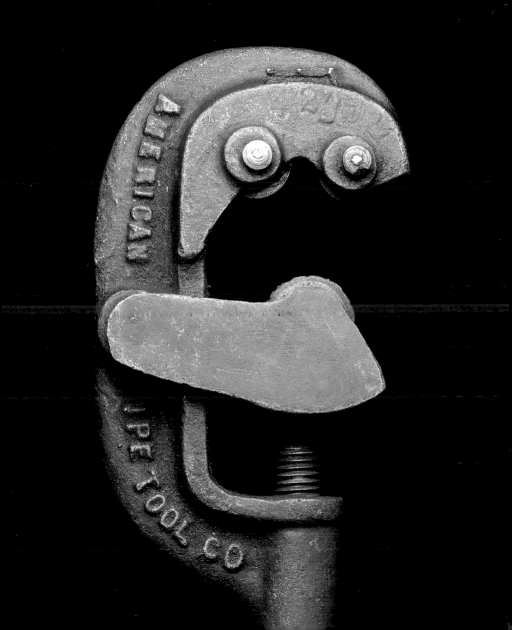

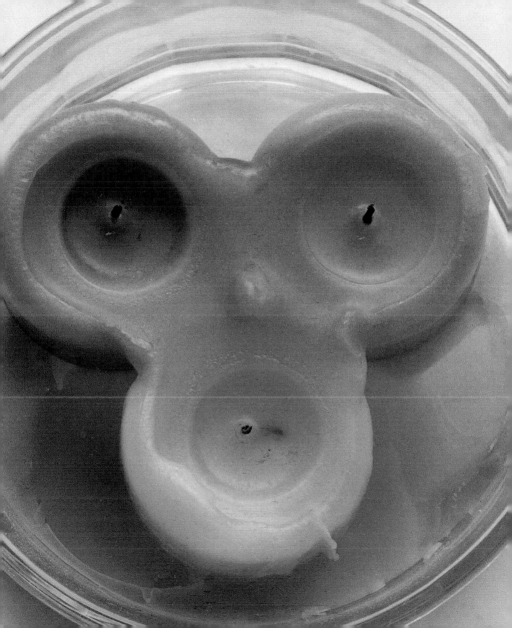

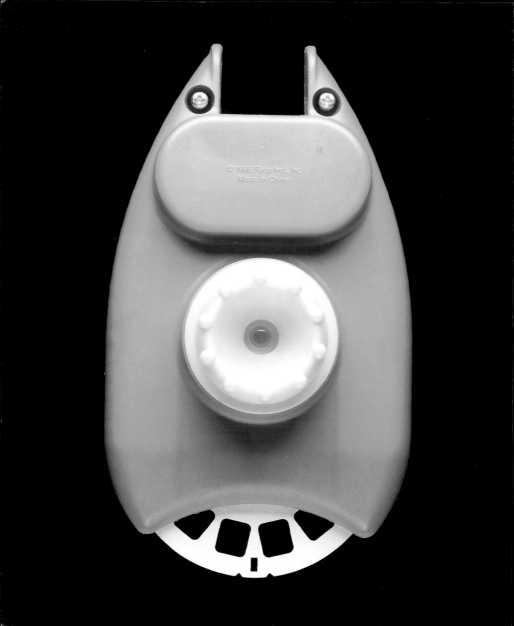

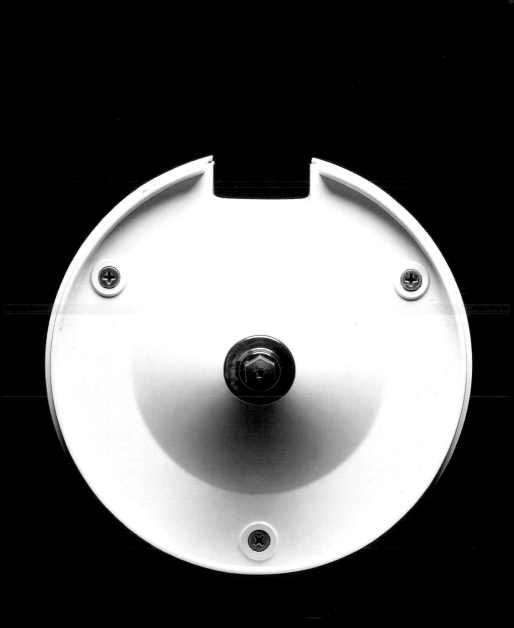

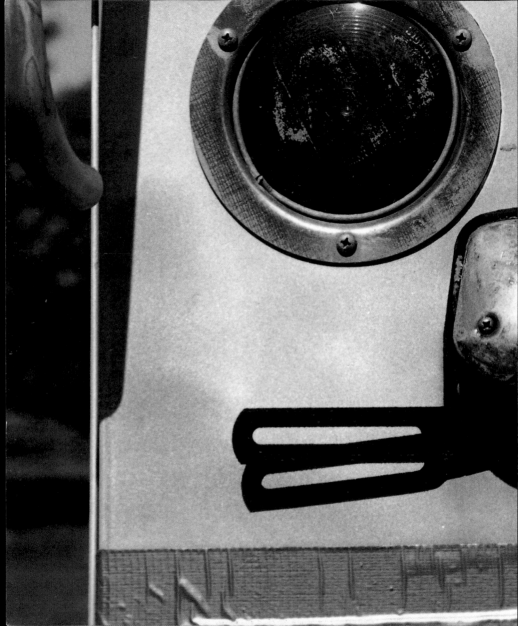

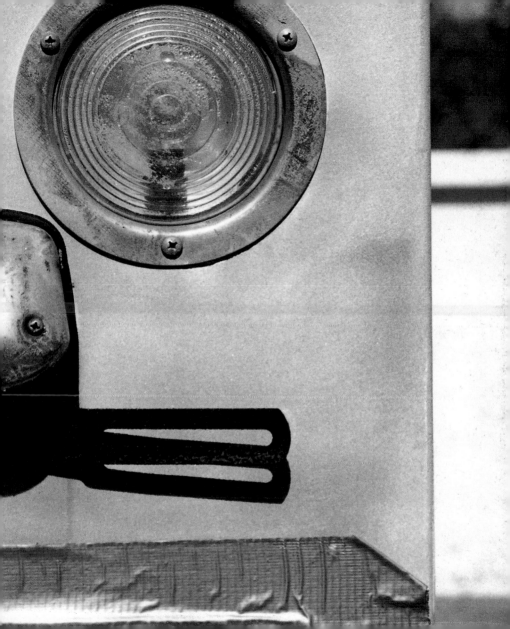

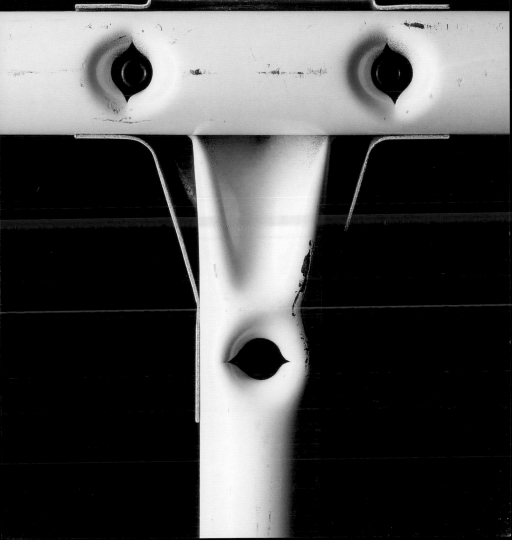

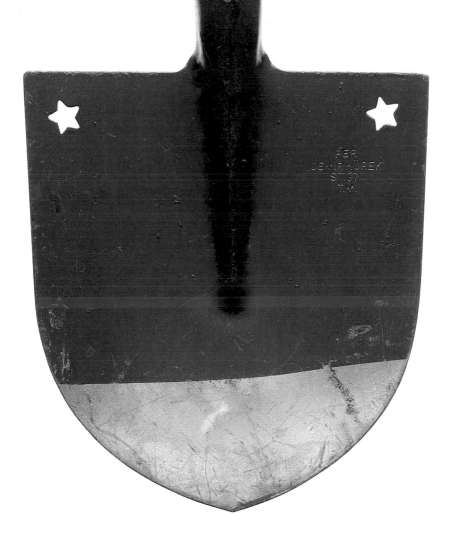

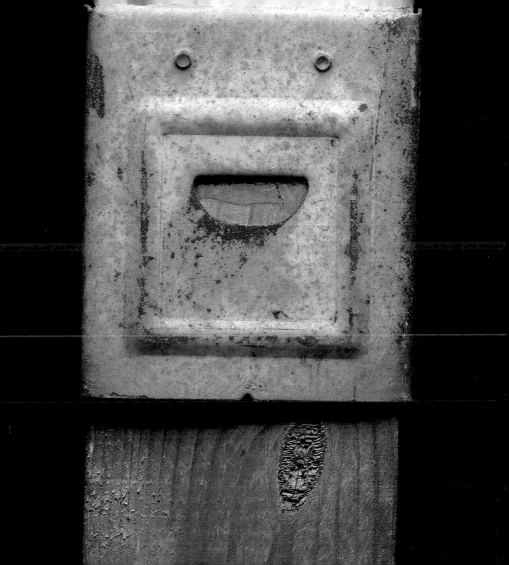

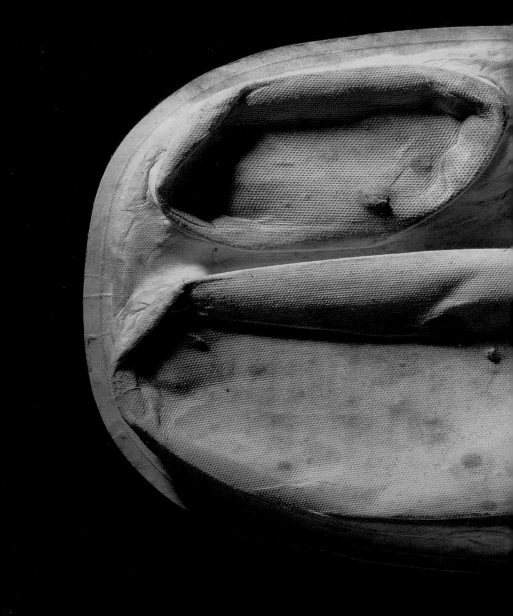

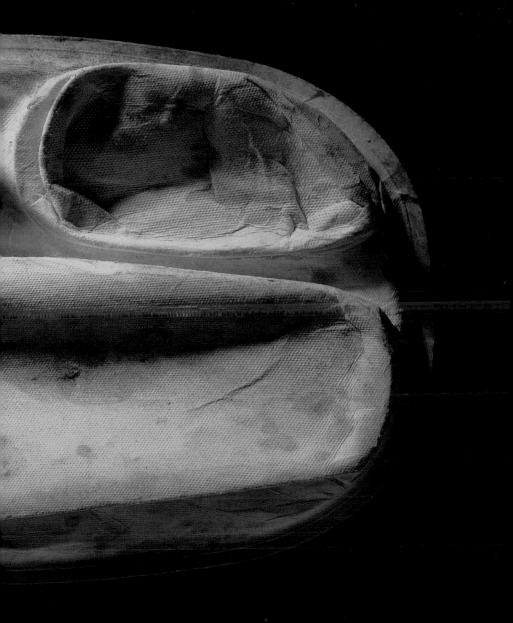

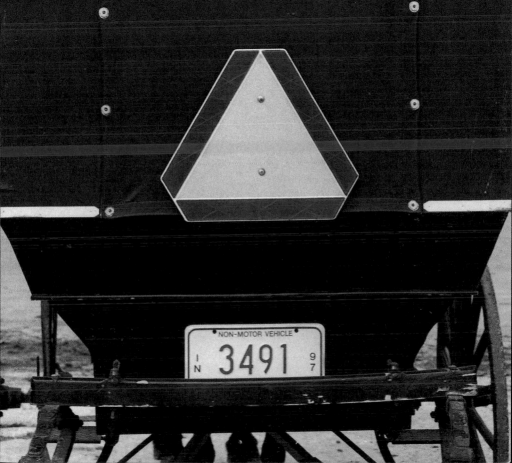

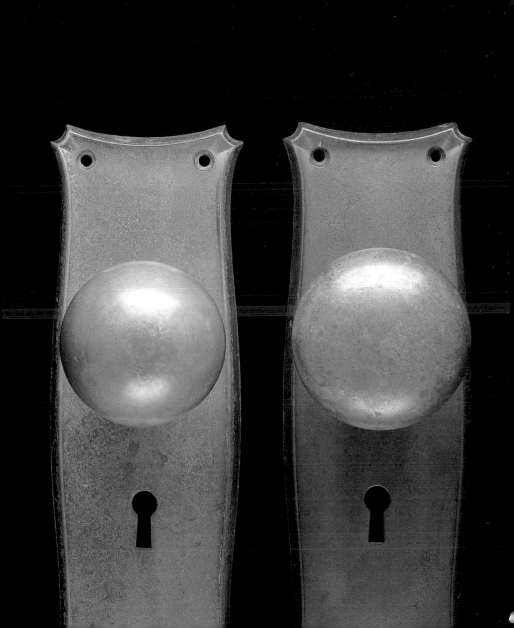

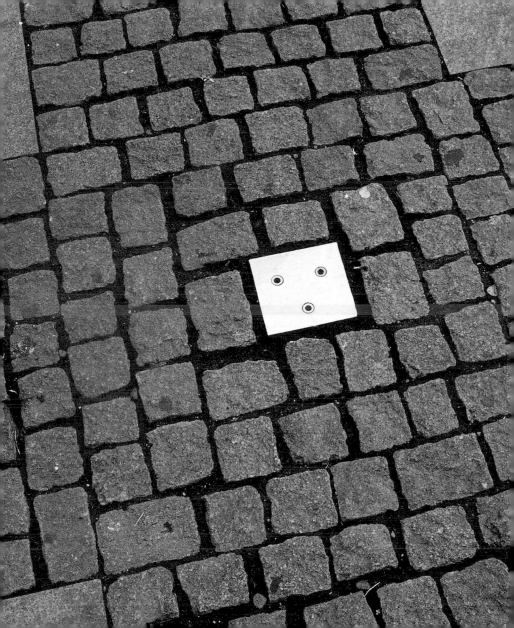

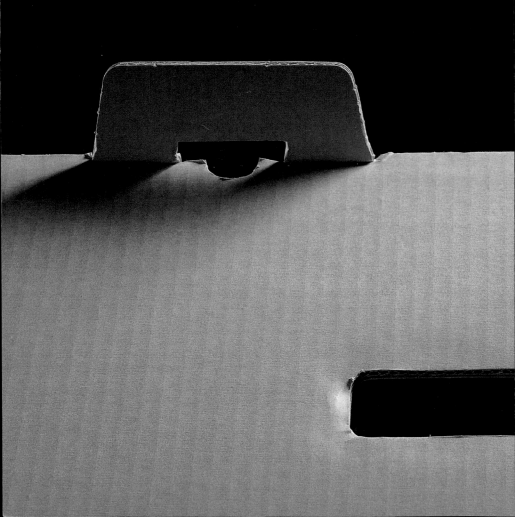

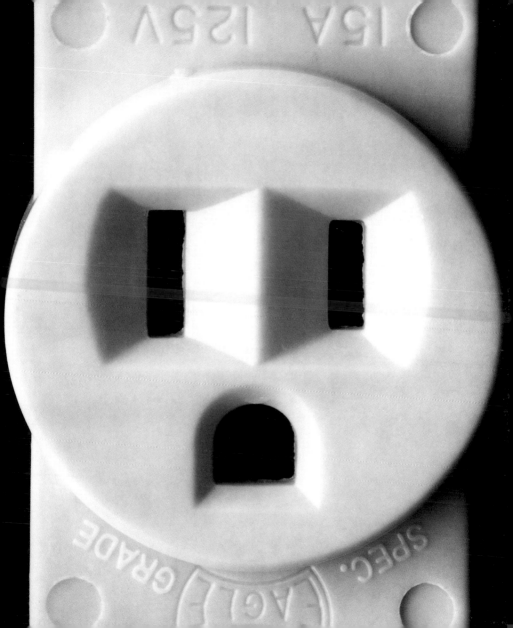

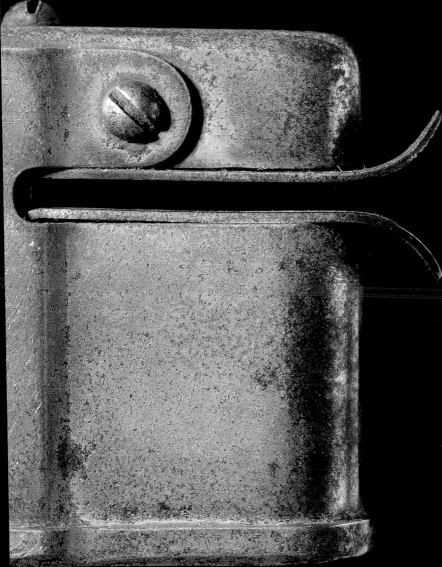

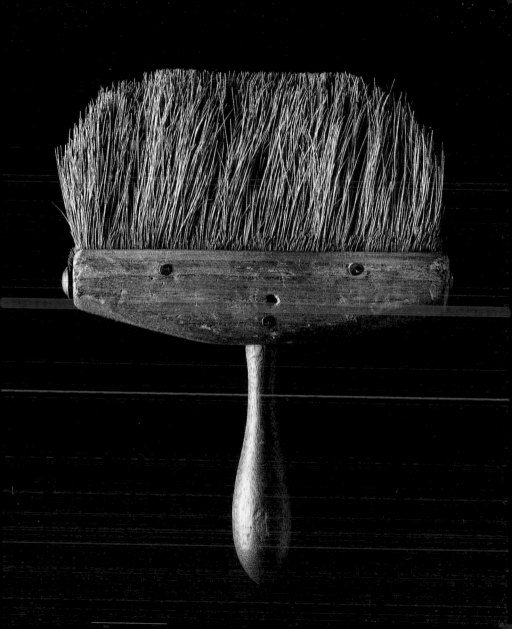

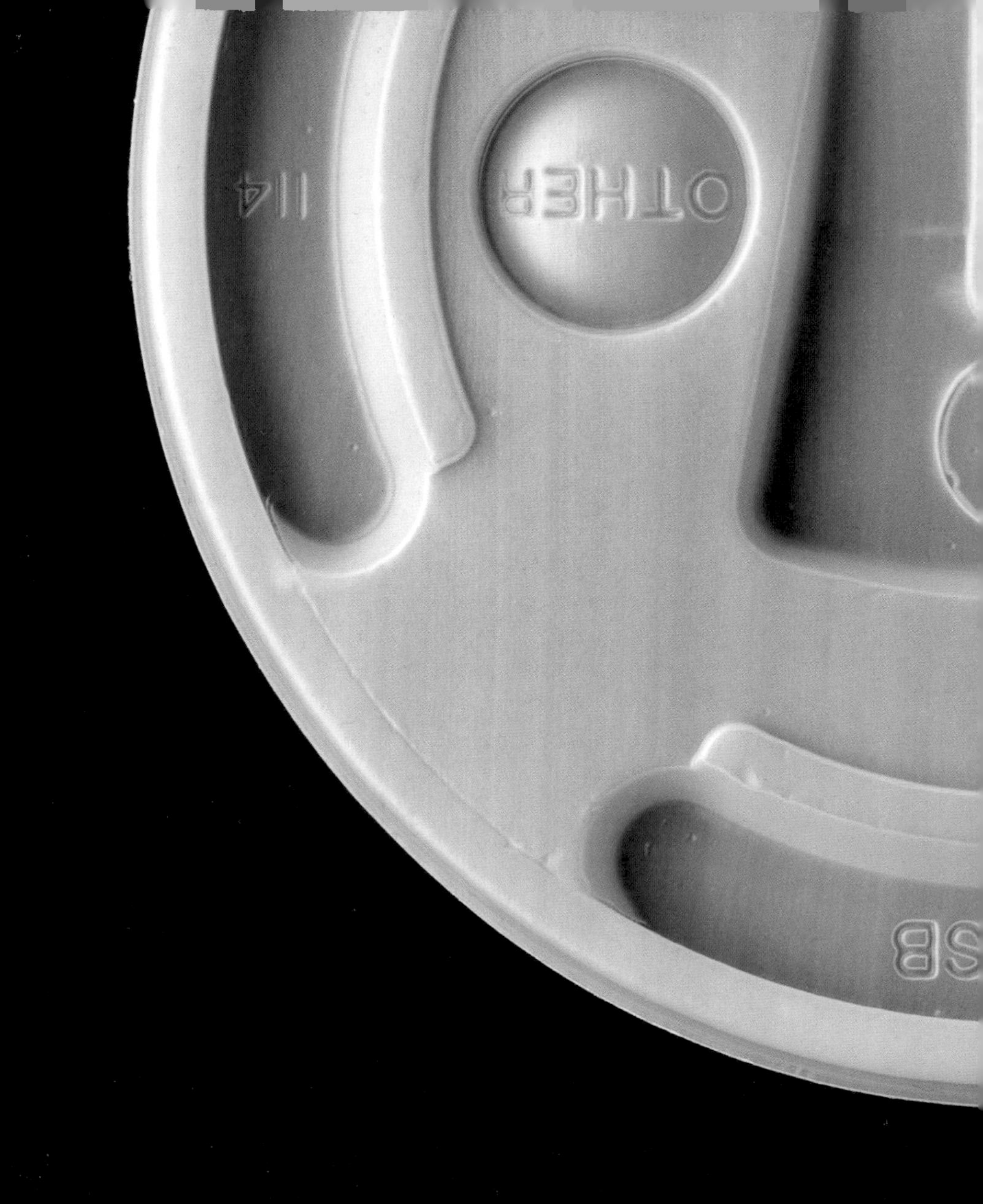
OTHER

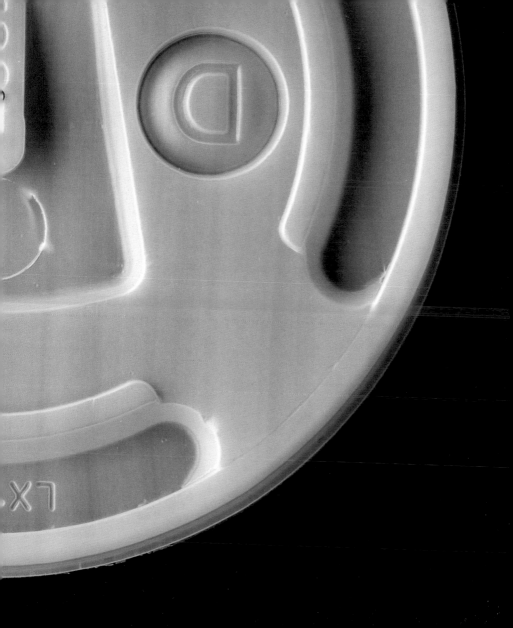

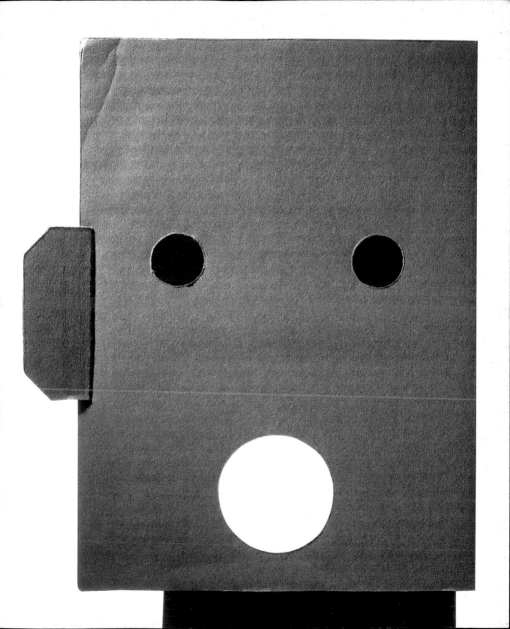

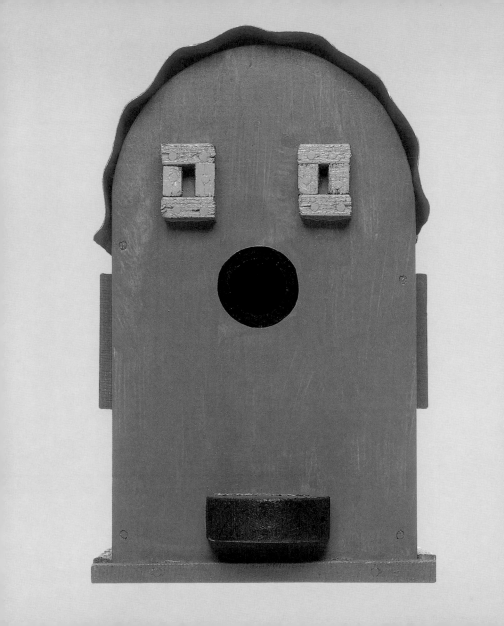

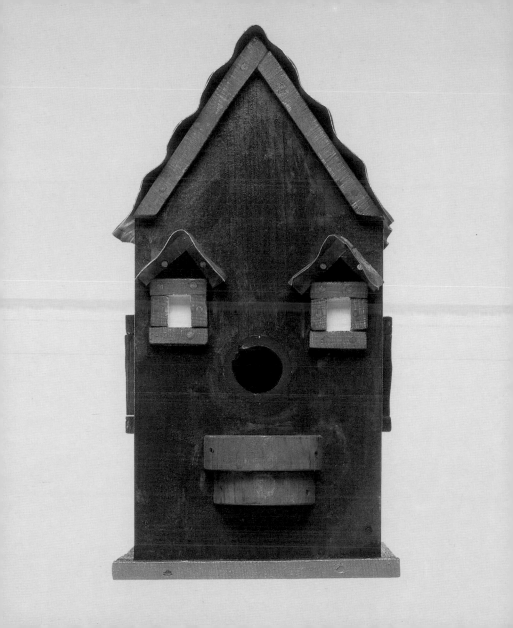

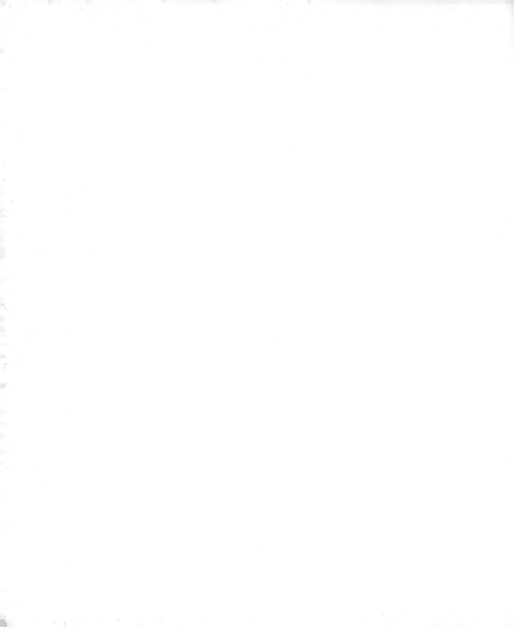

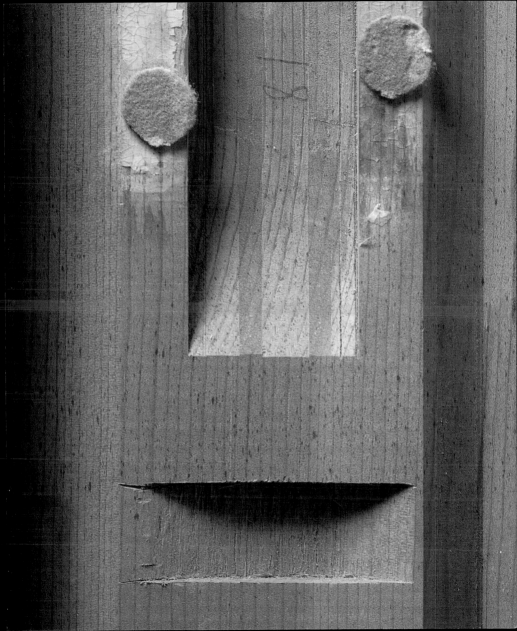

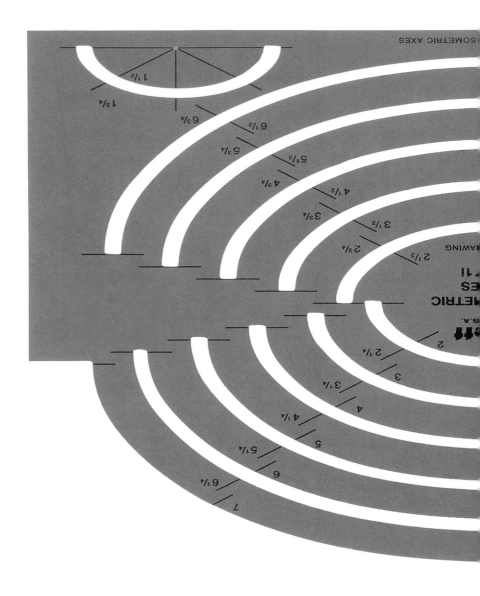

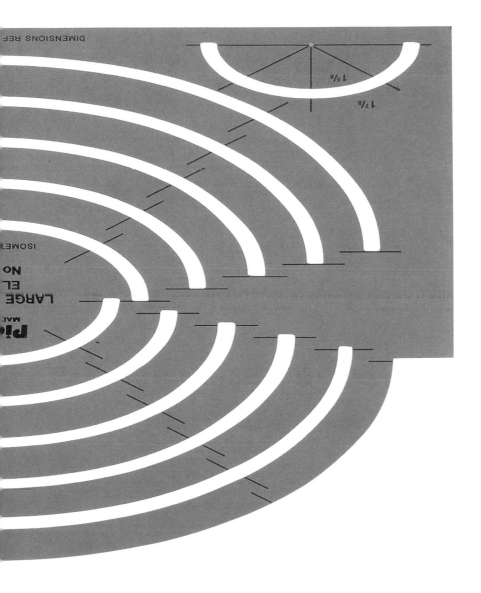

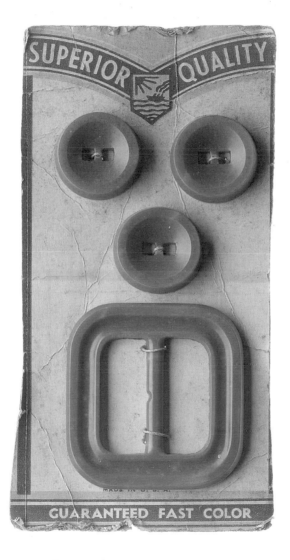

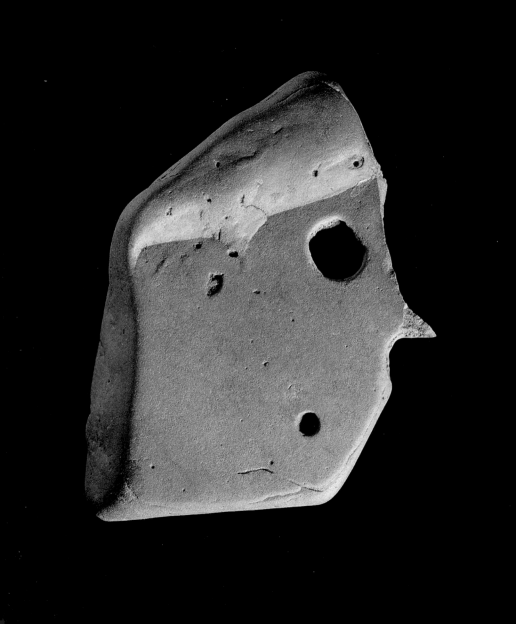

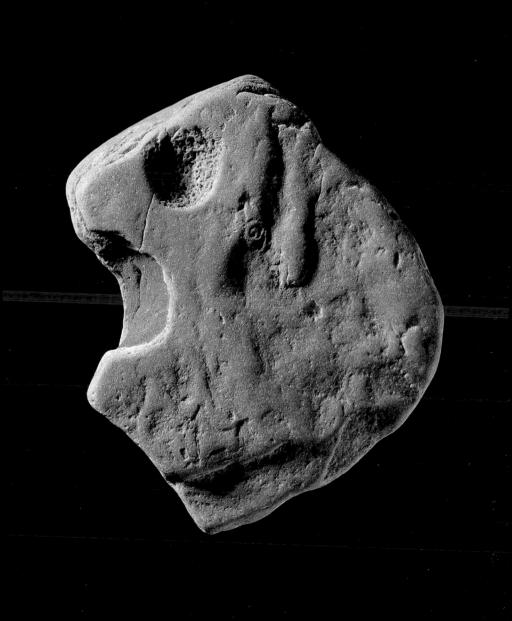

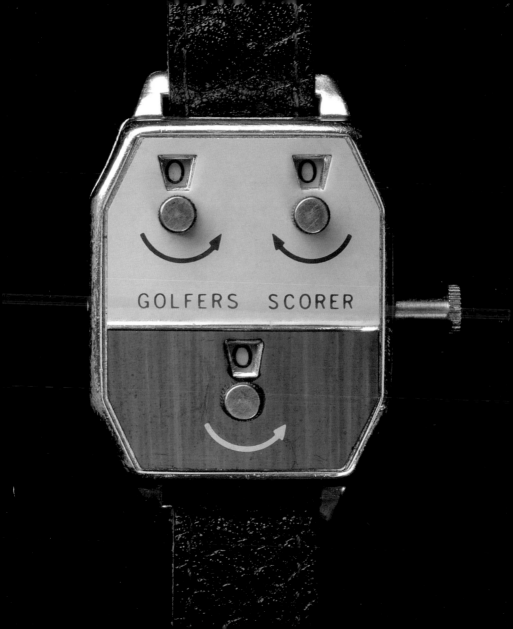

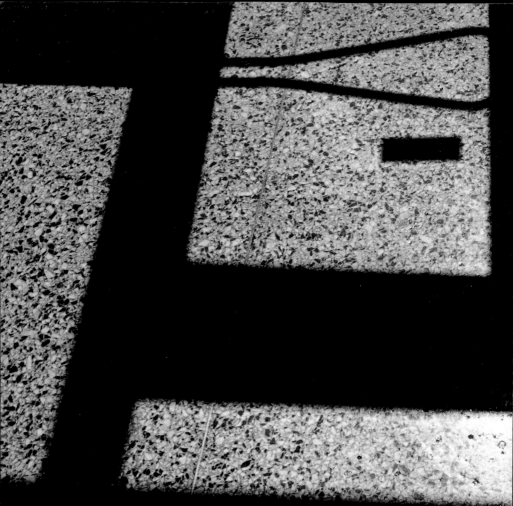

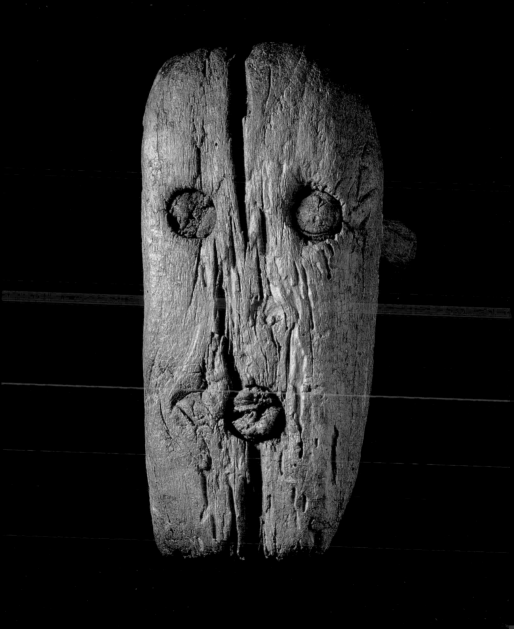

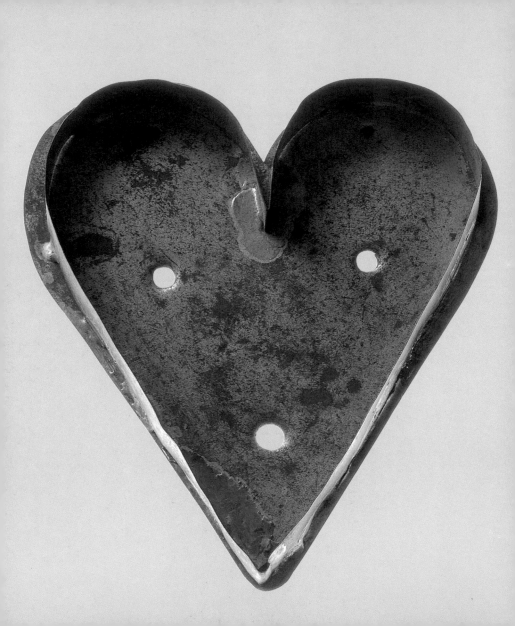

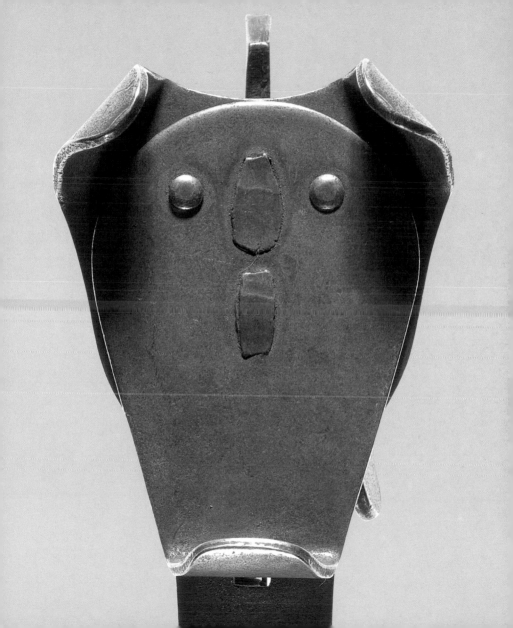

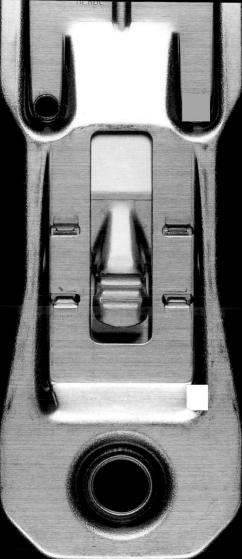

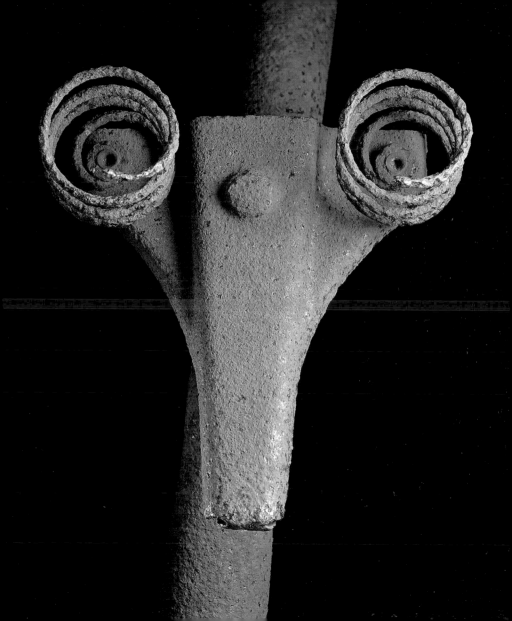

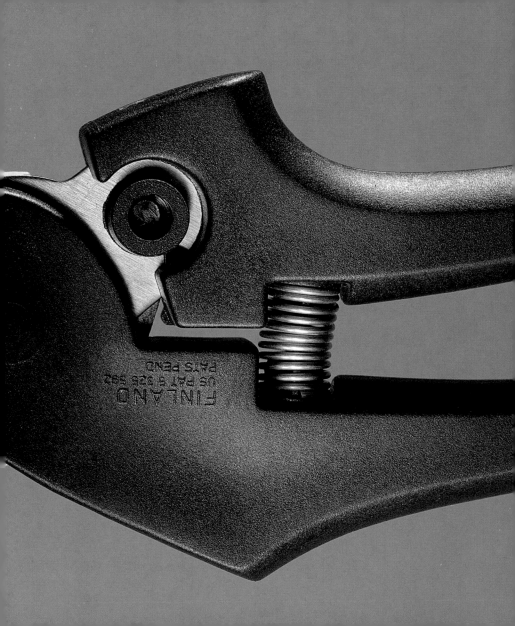

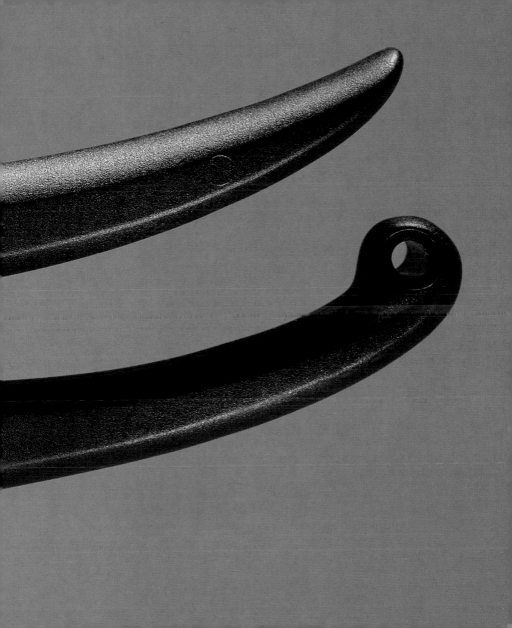

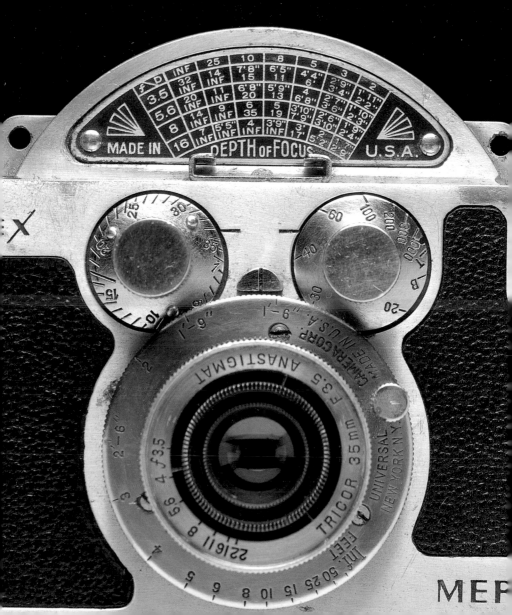

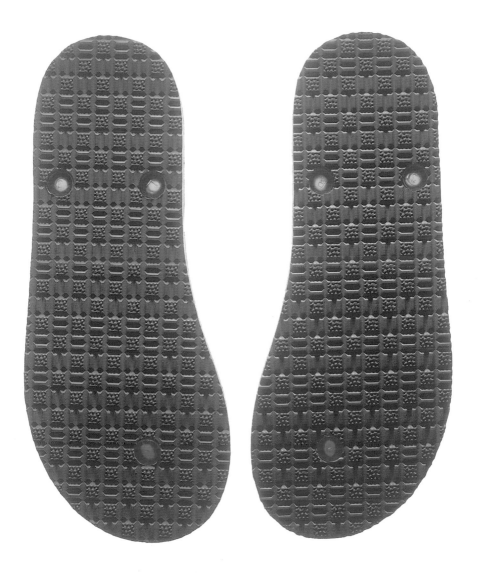

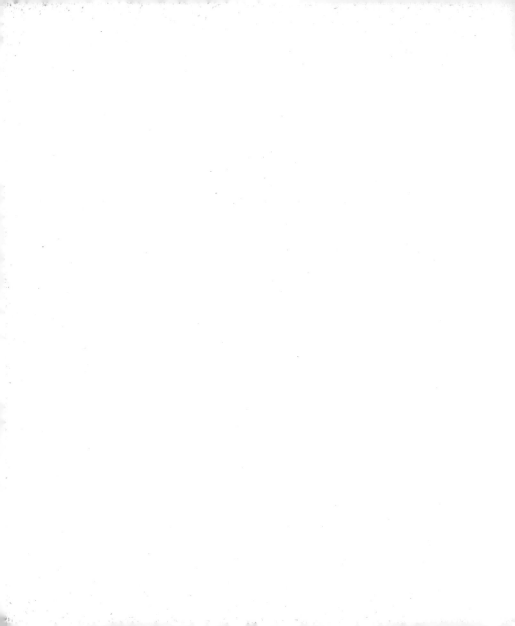

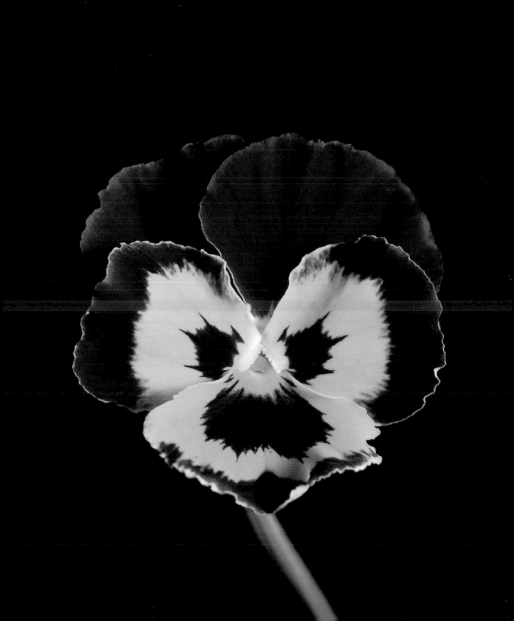

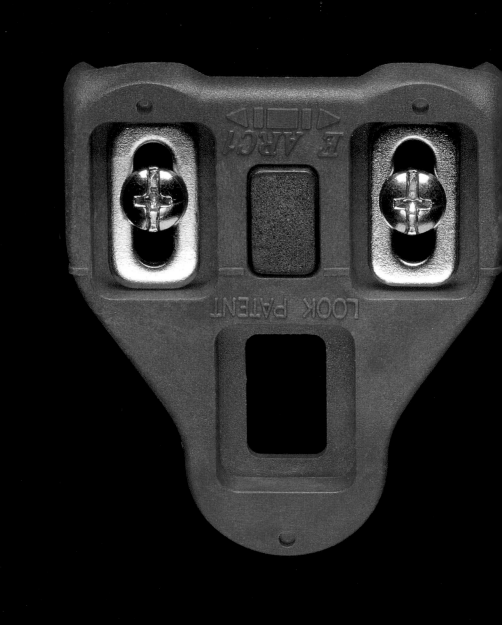

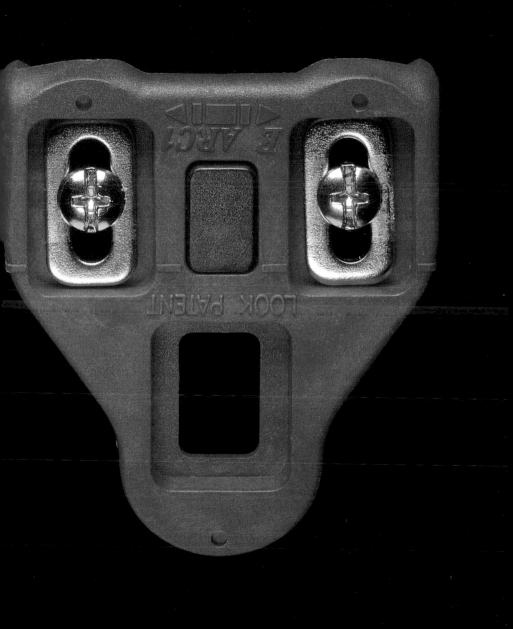

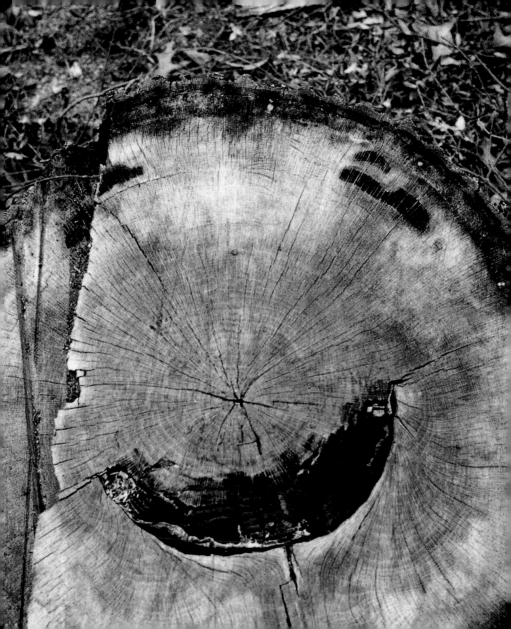

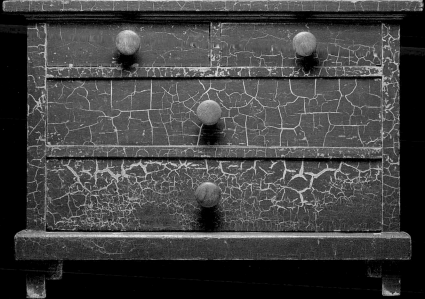

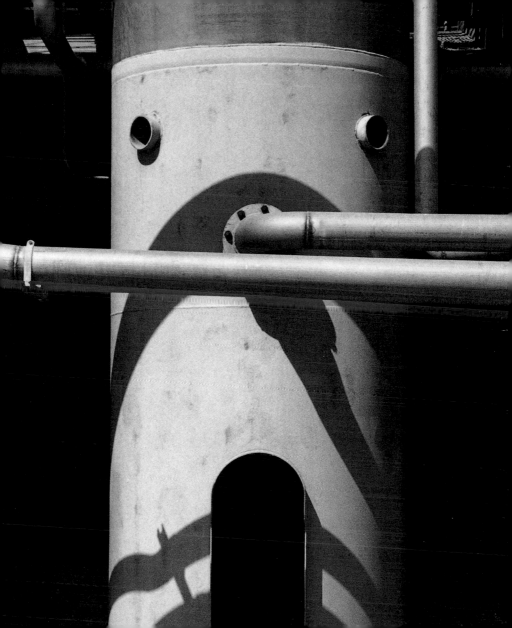

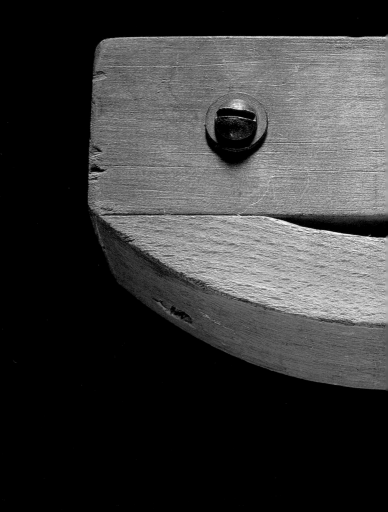

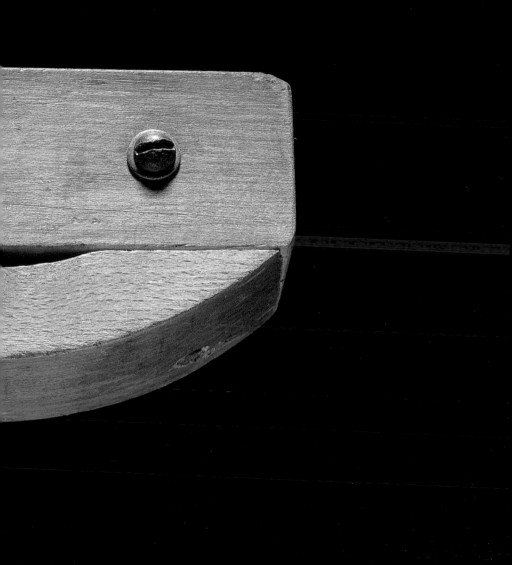

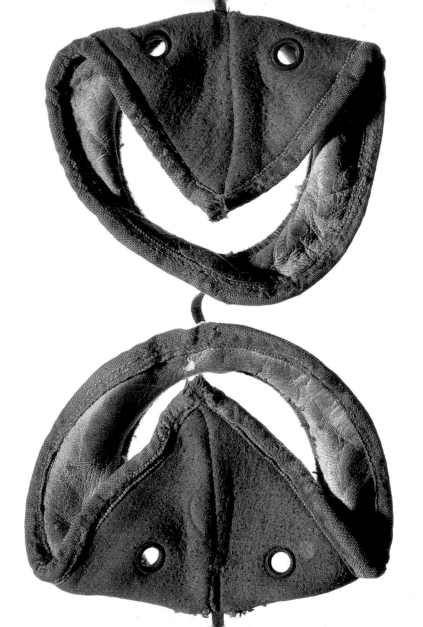

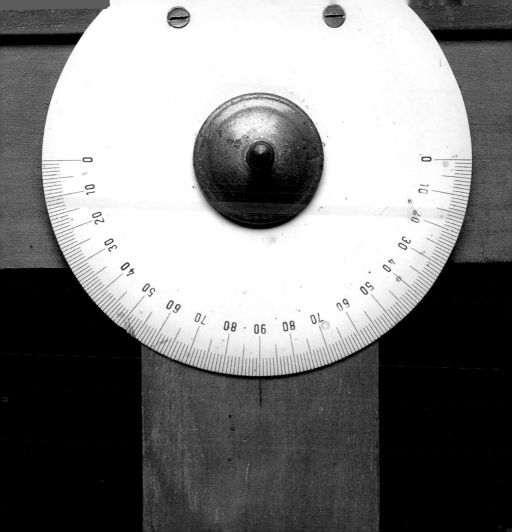

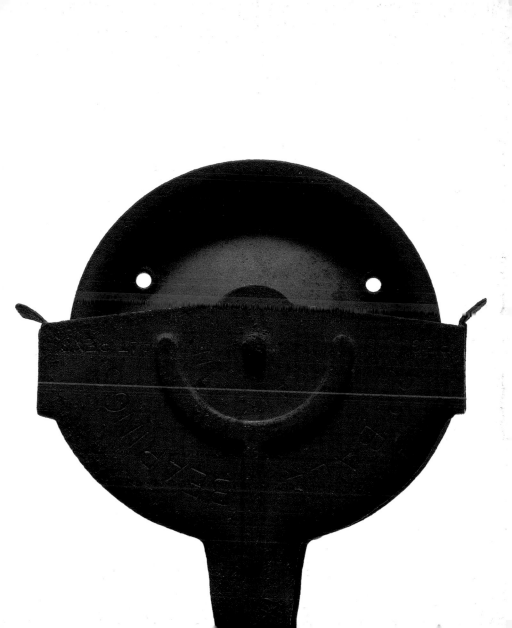

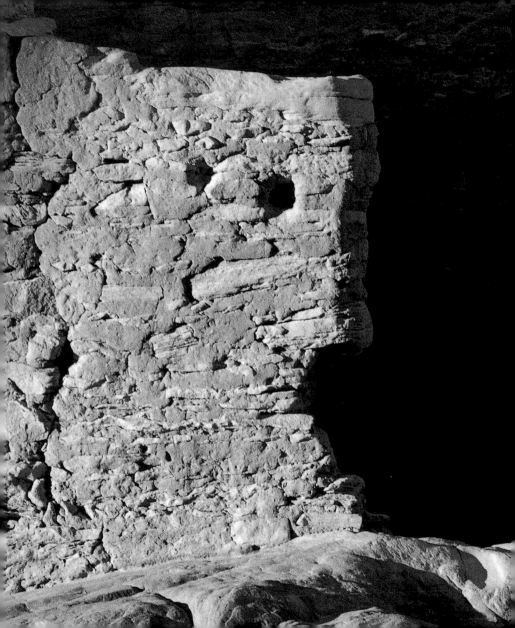

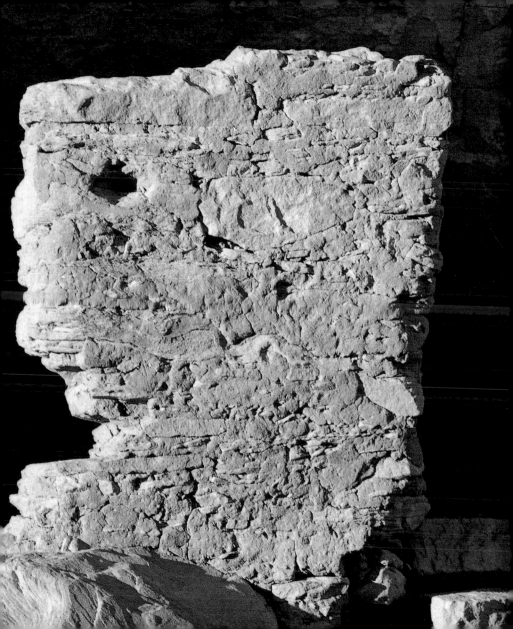

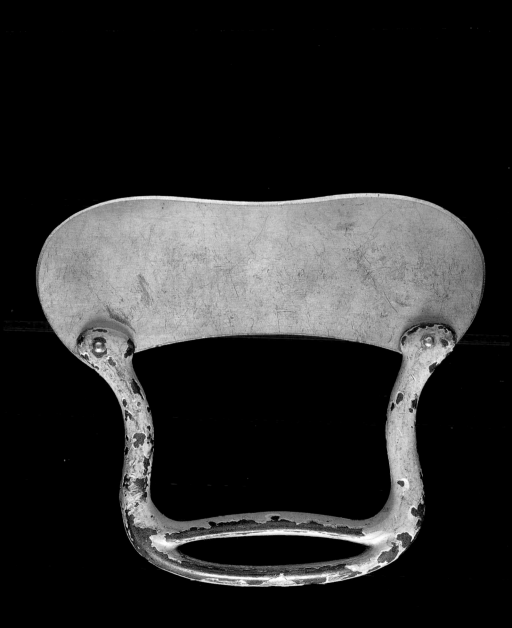

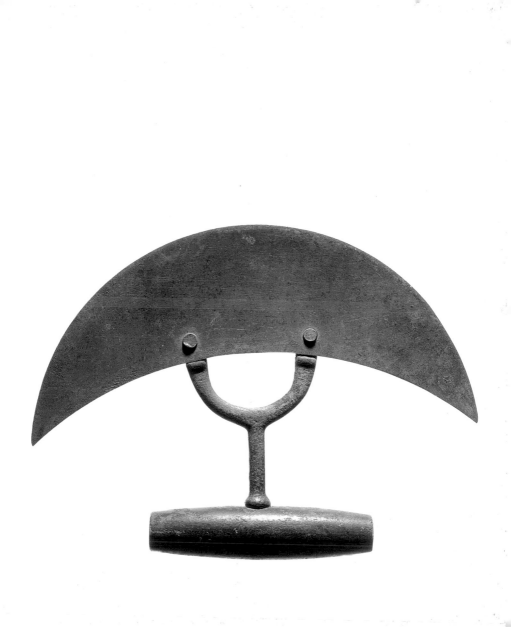

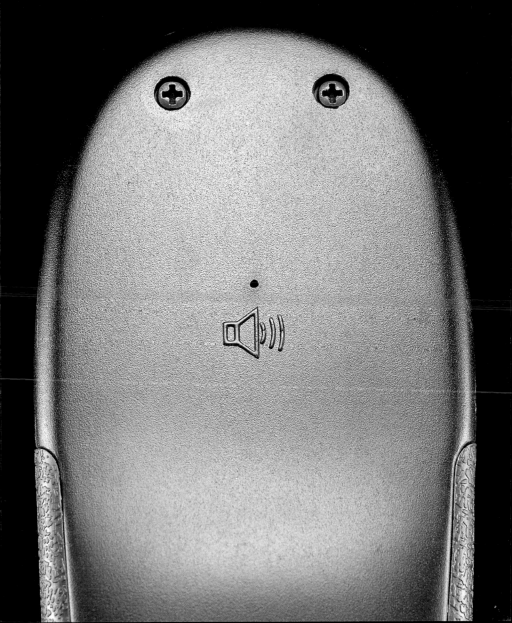

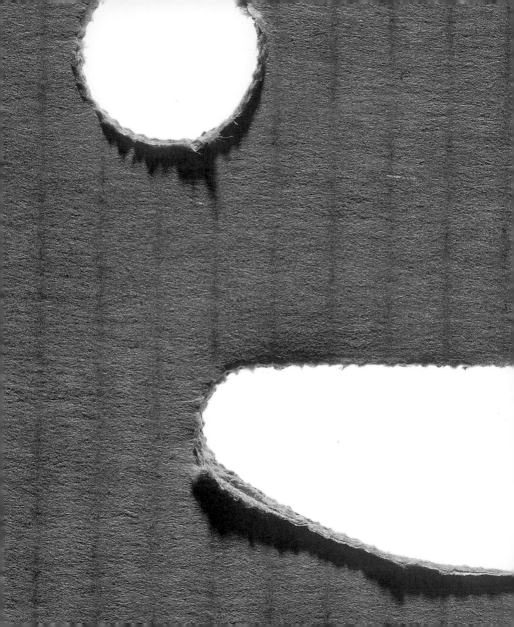

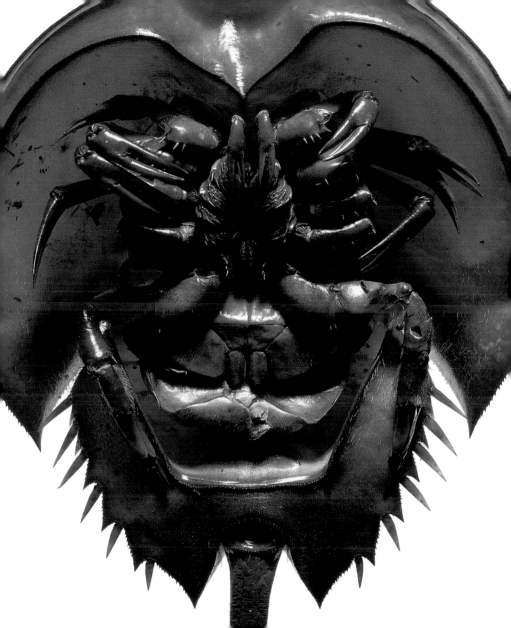

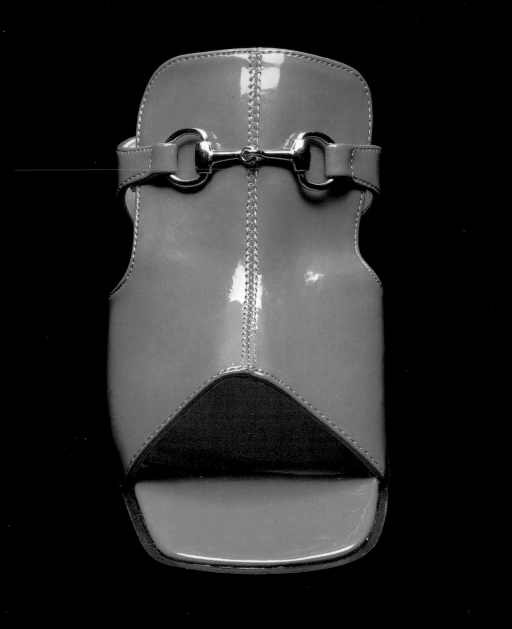

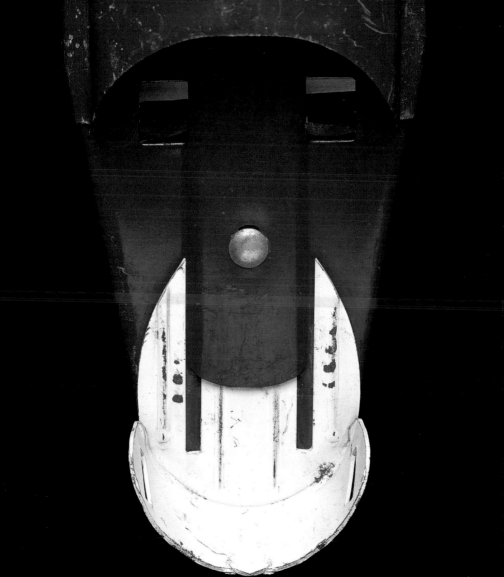

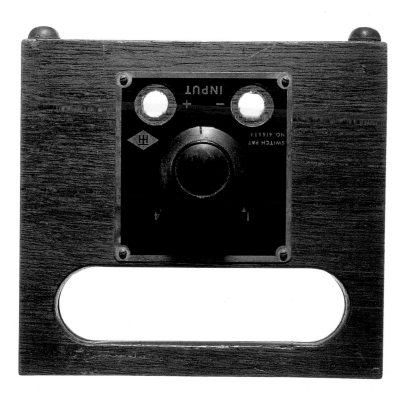

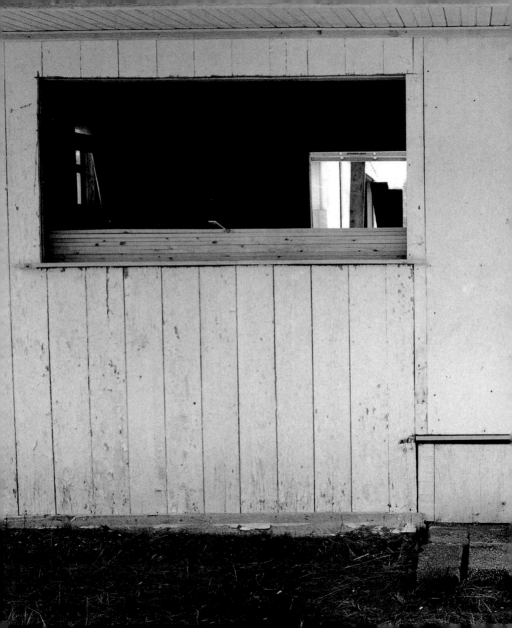

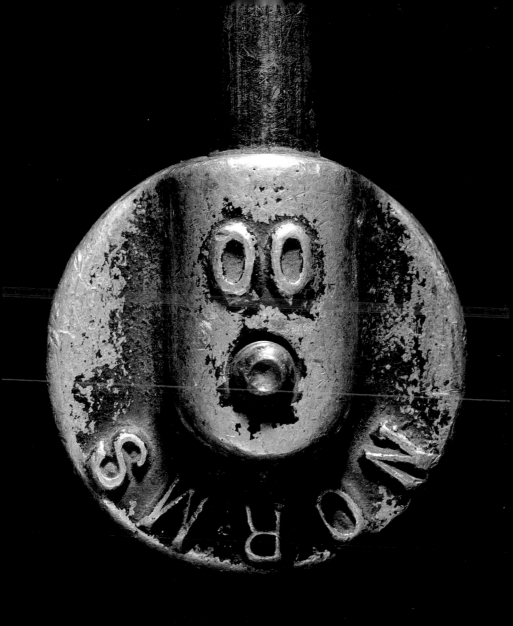

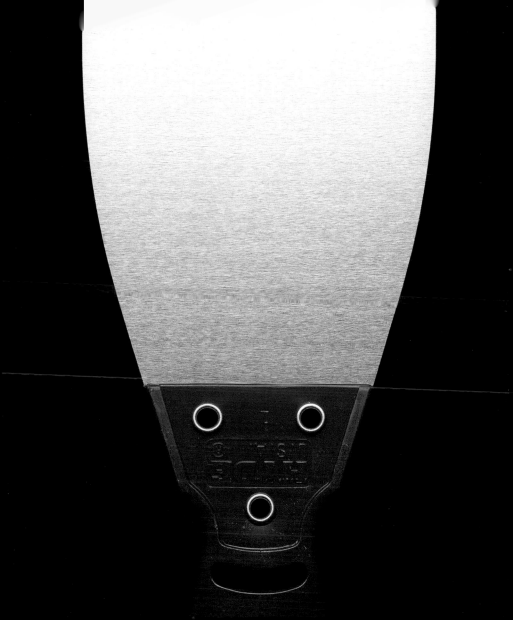

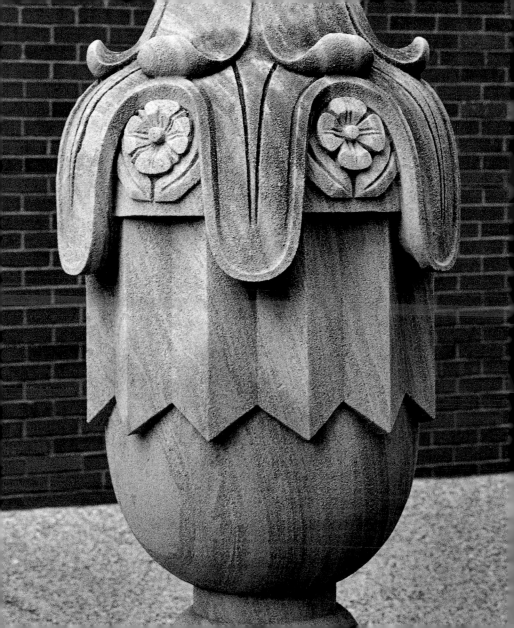

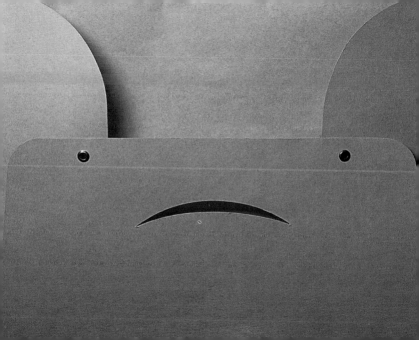

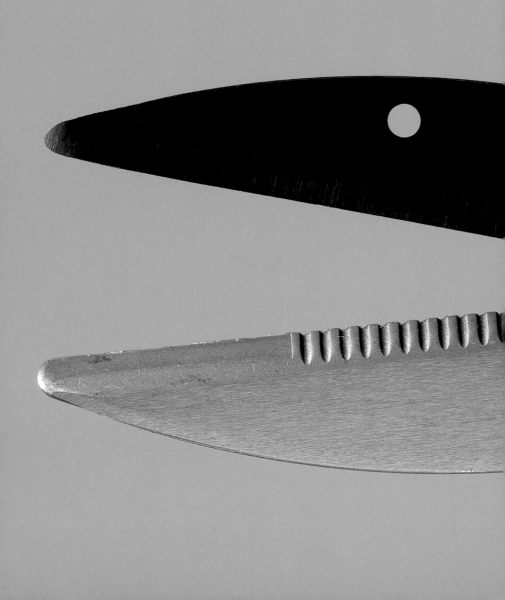

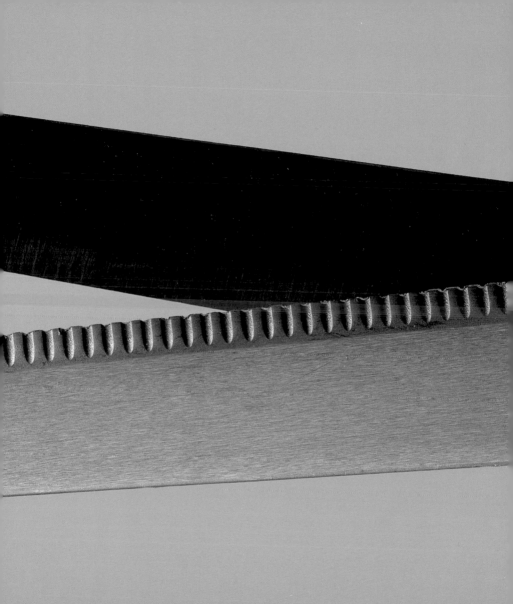

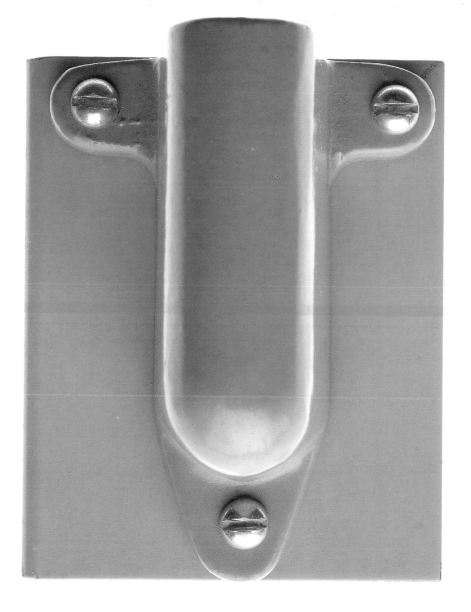

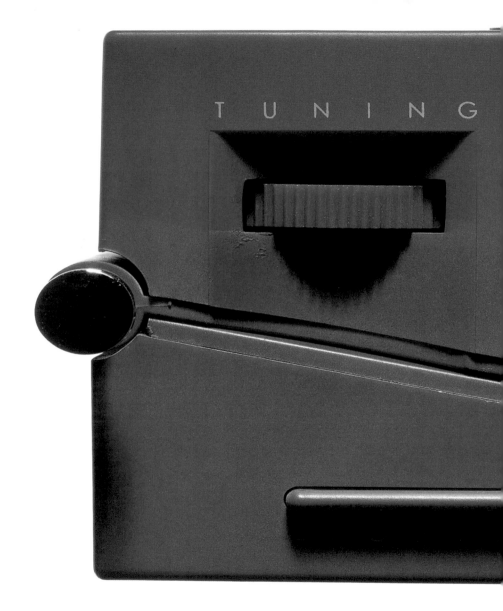

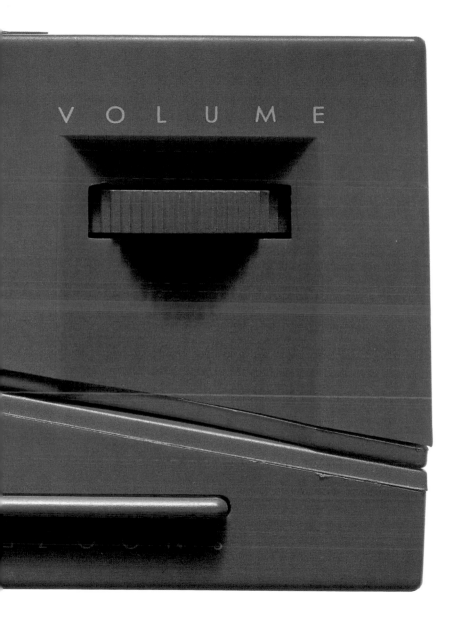

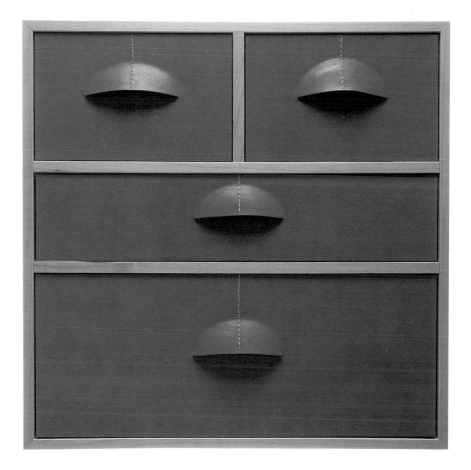

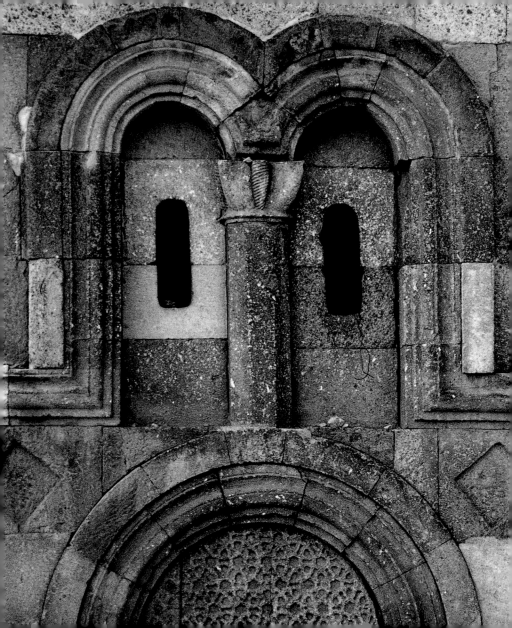

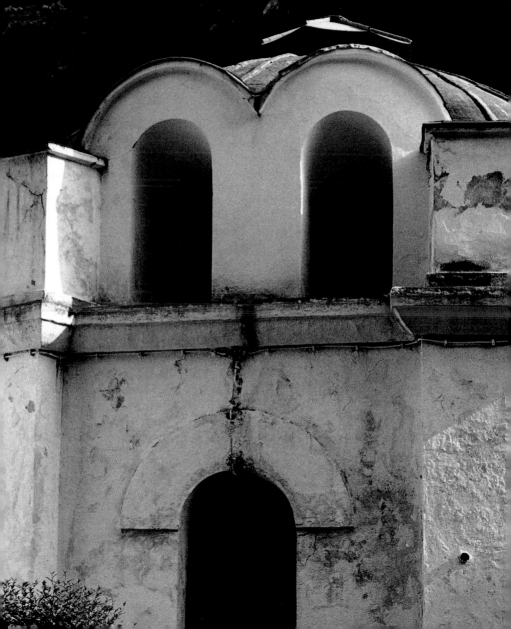

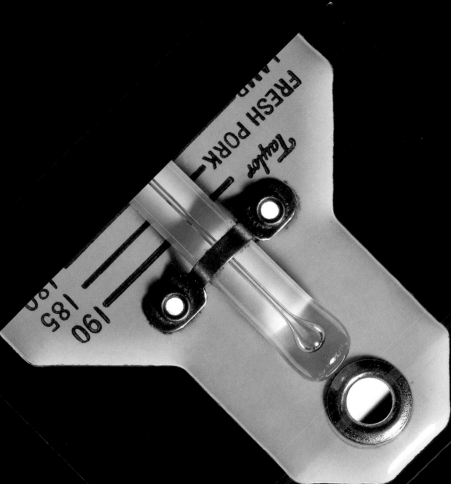

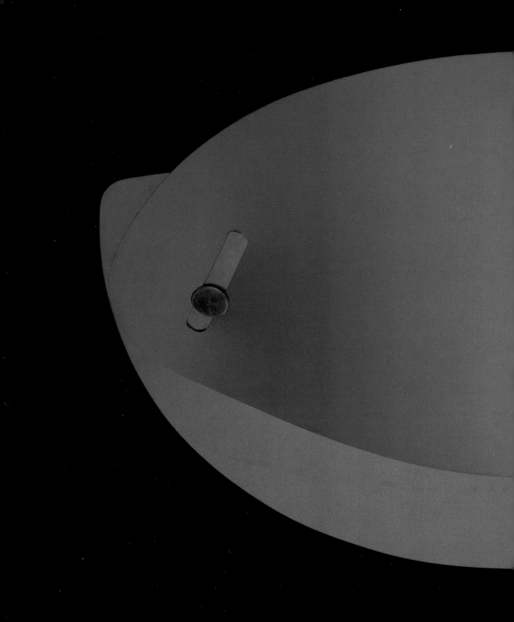

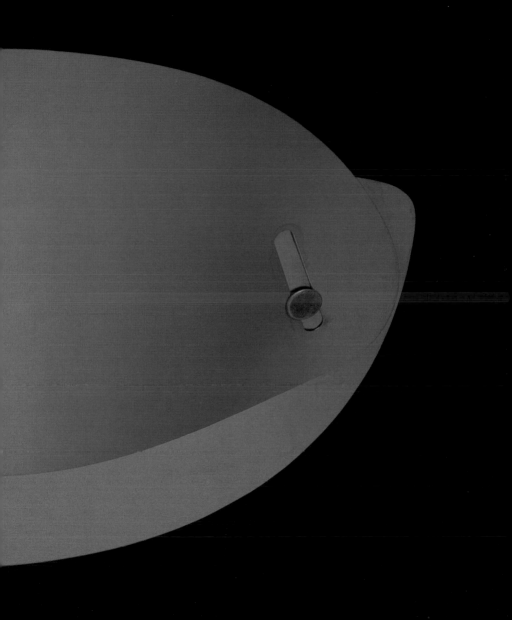

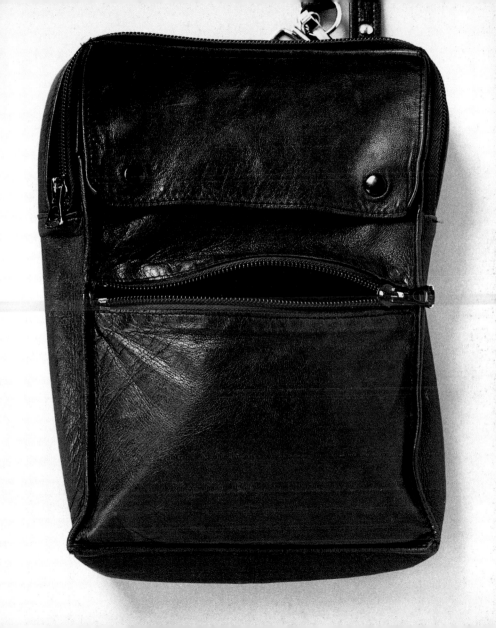

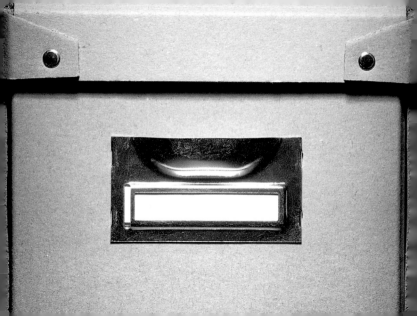

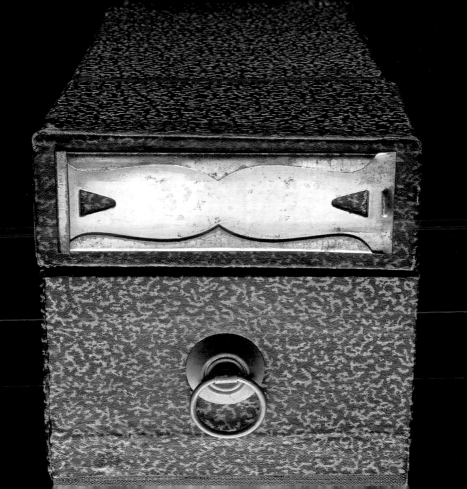

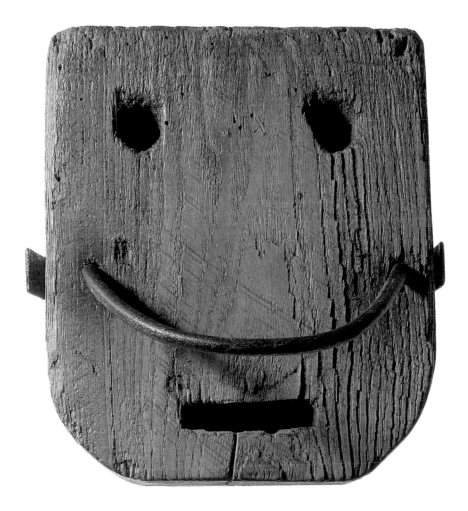

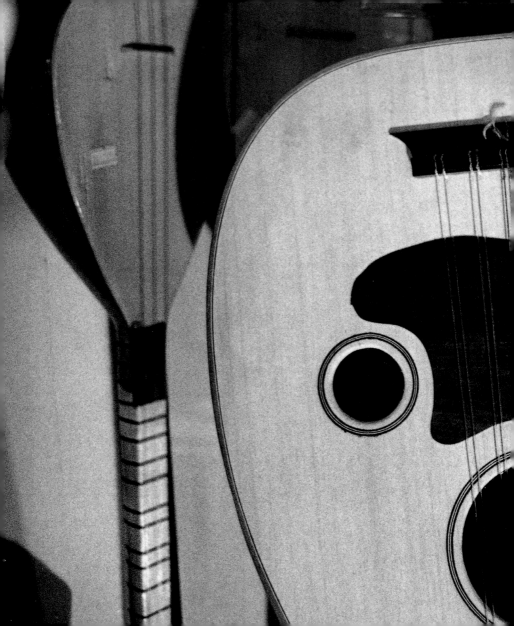

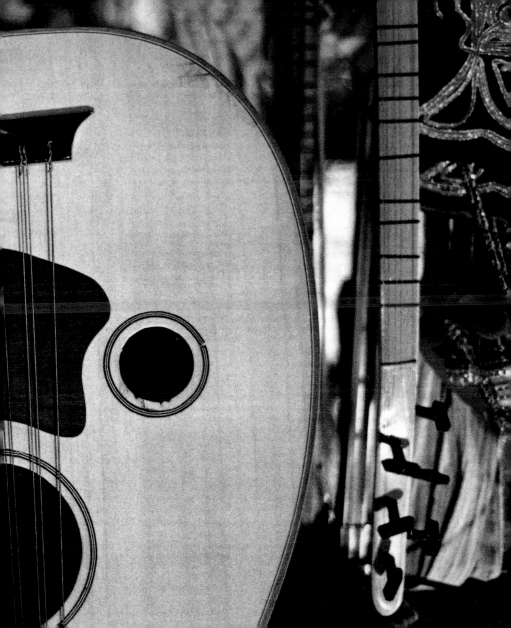

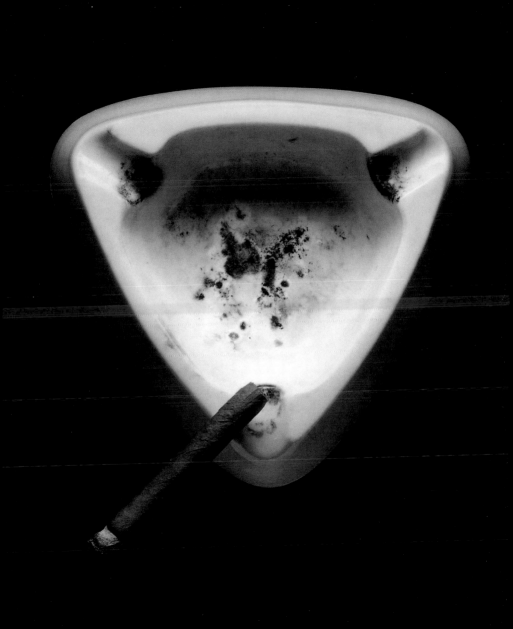

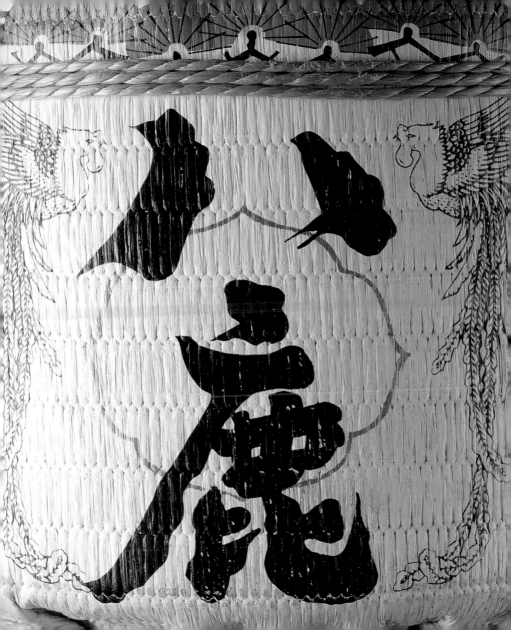

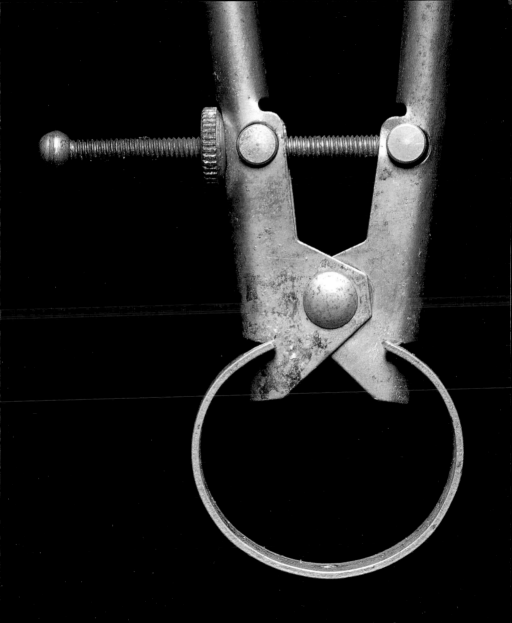

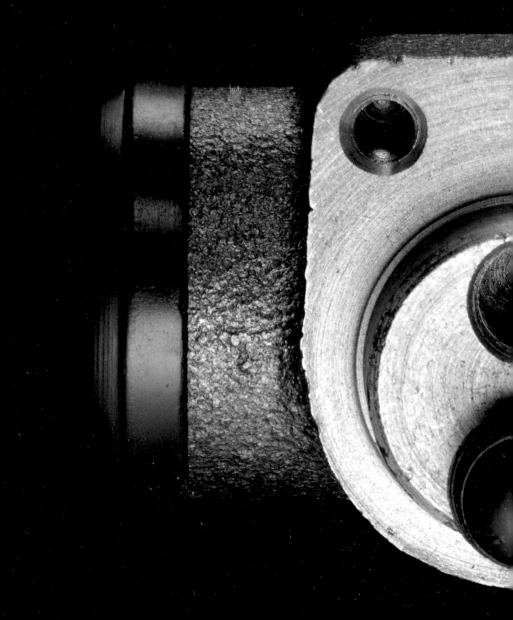

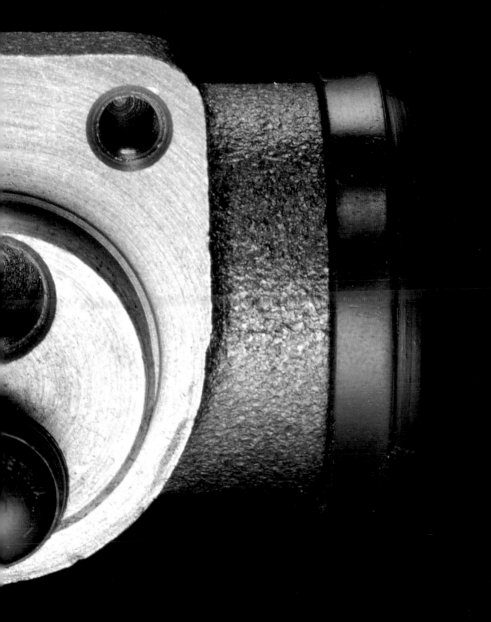

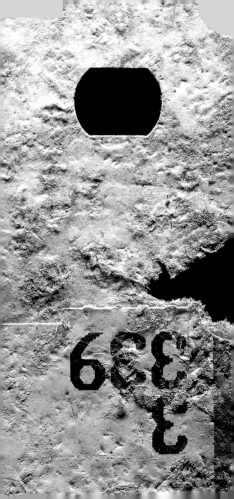

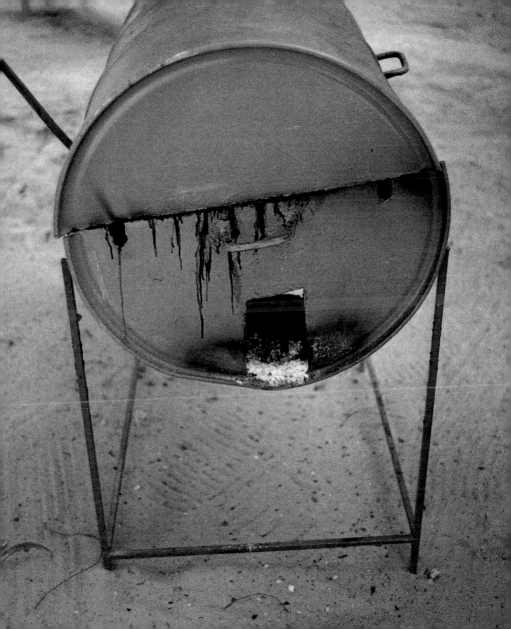

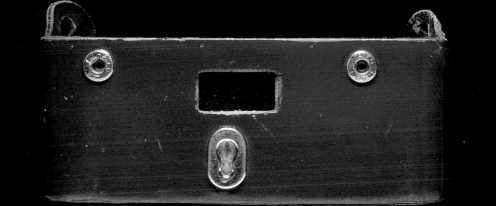

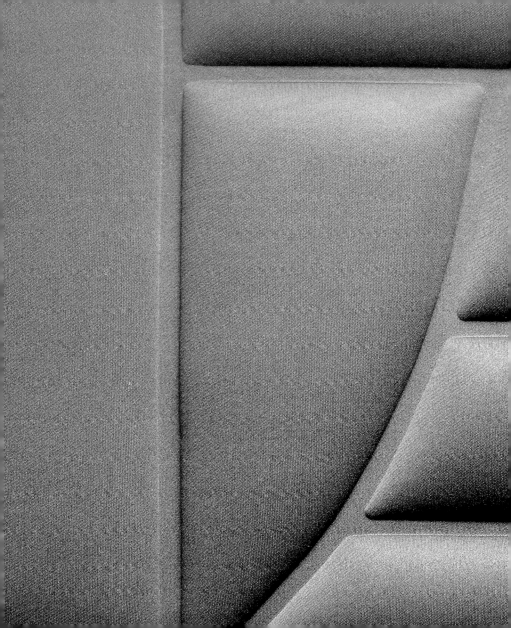

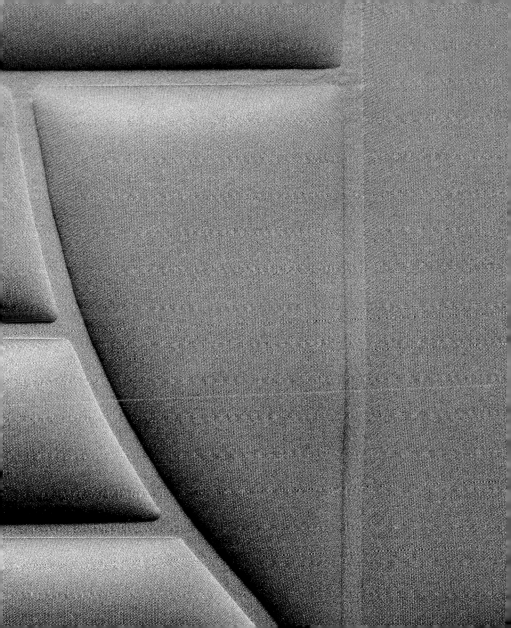

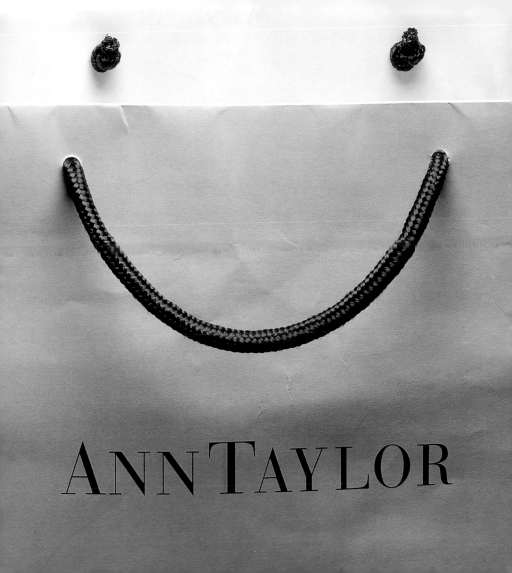

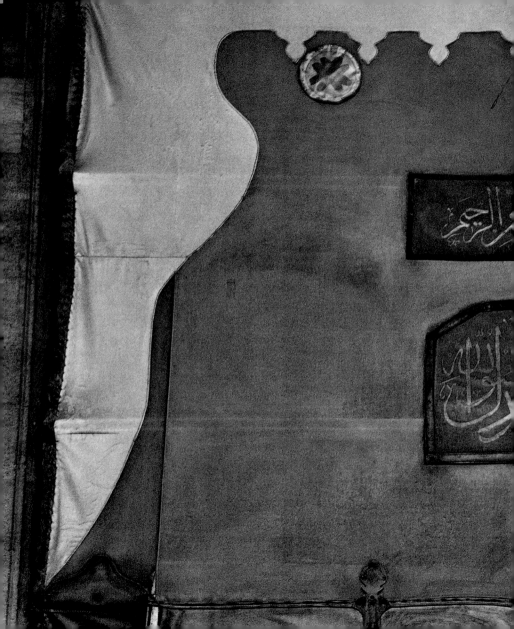

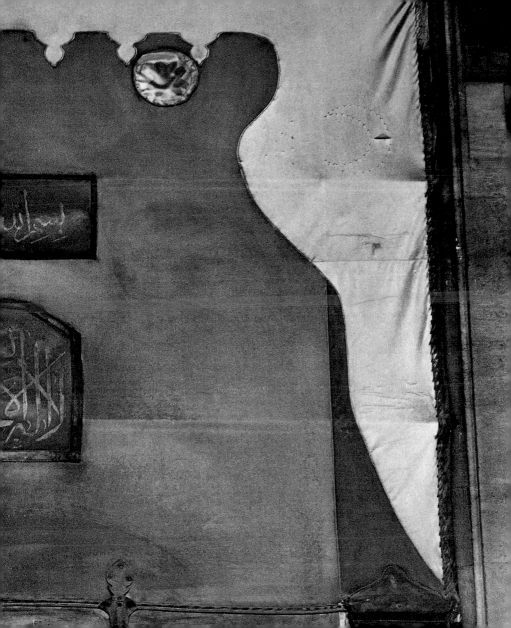

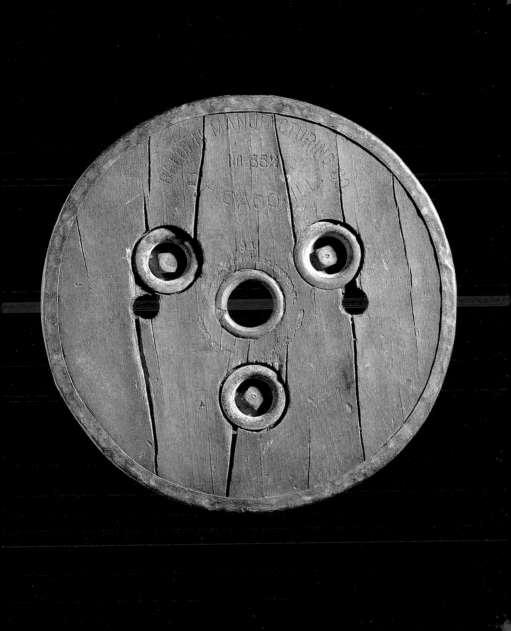

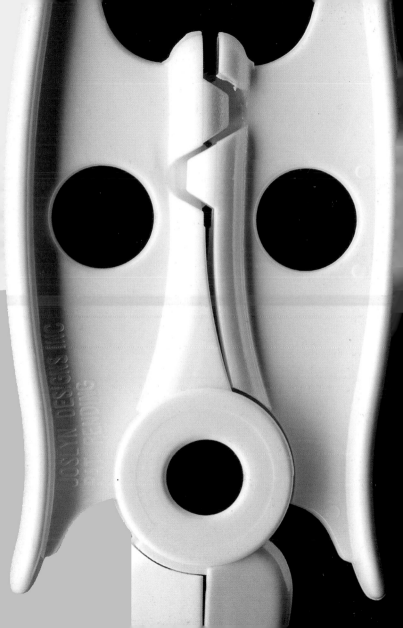

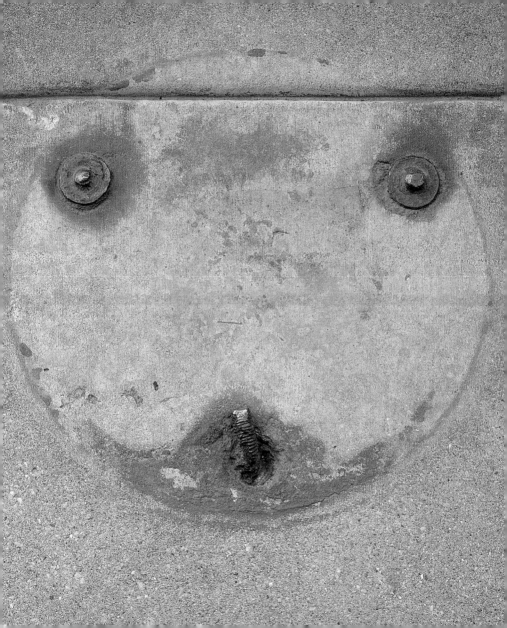

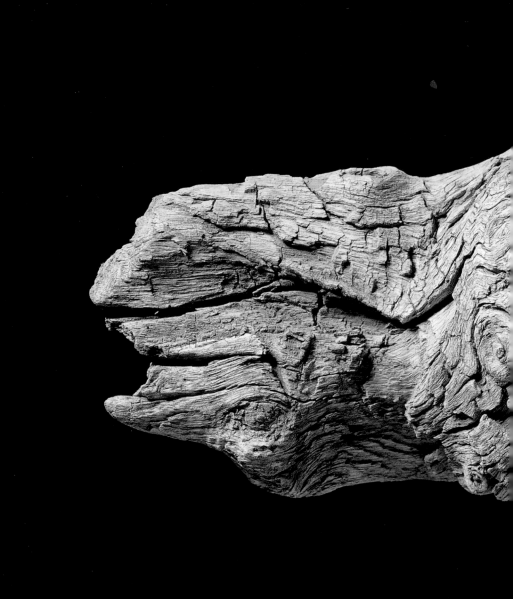

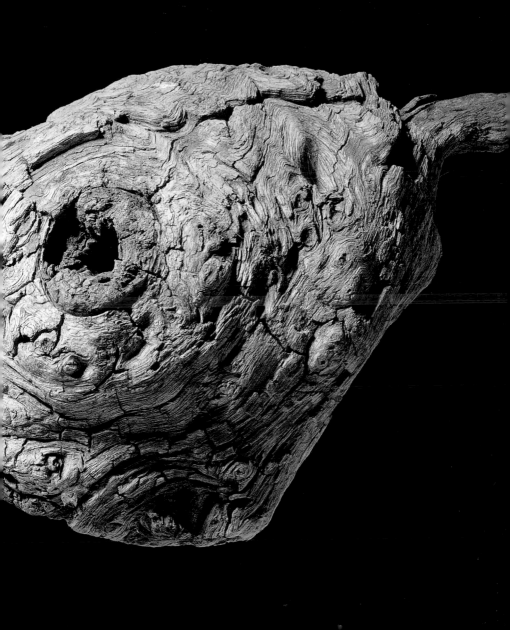

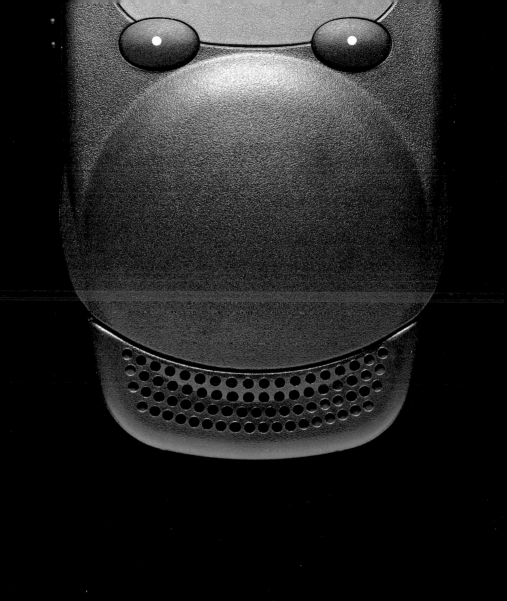

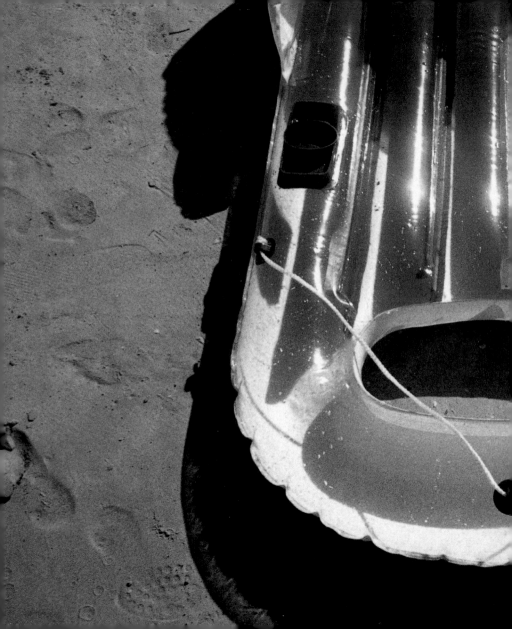

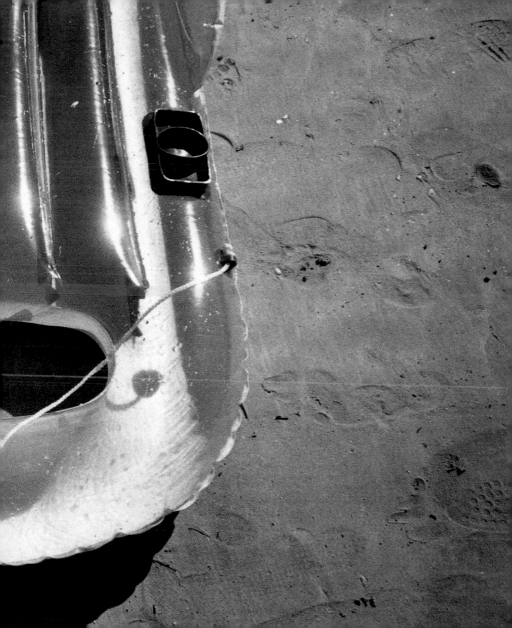

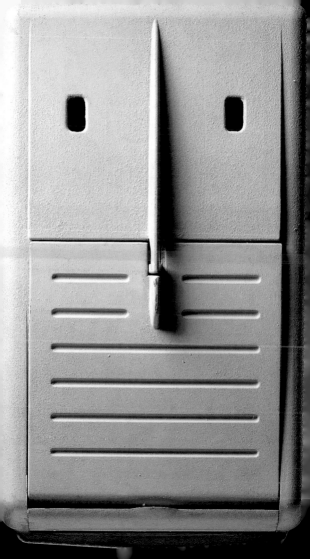

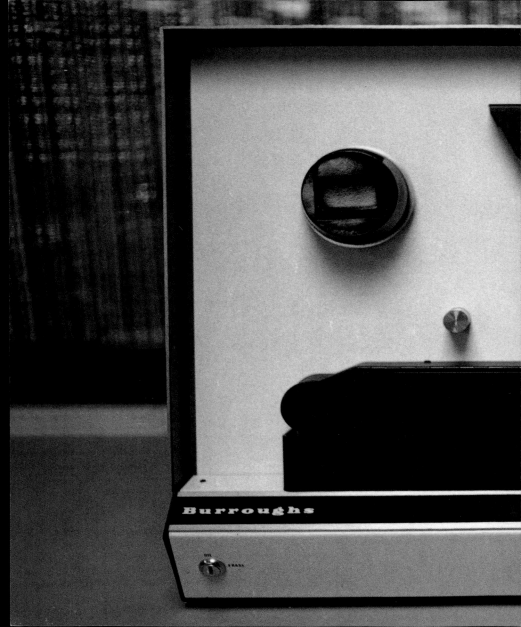

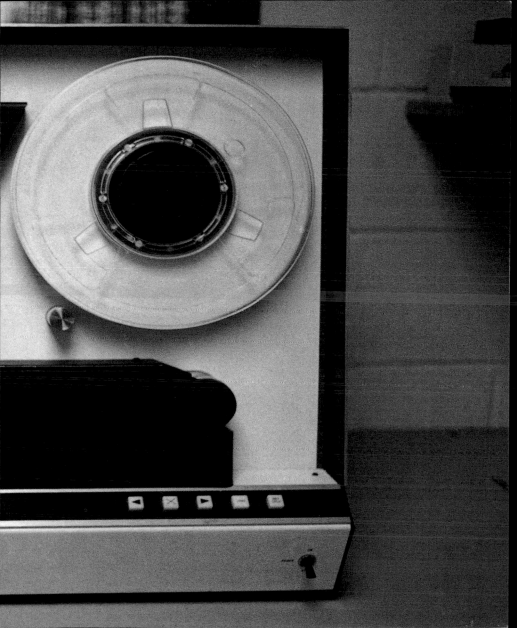

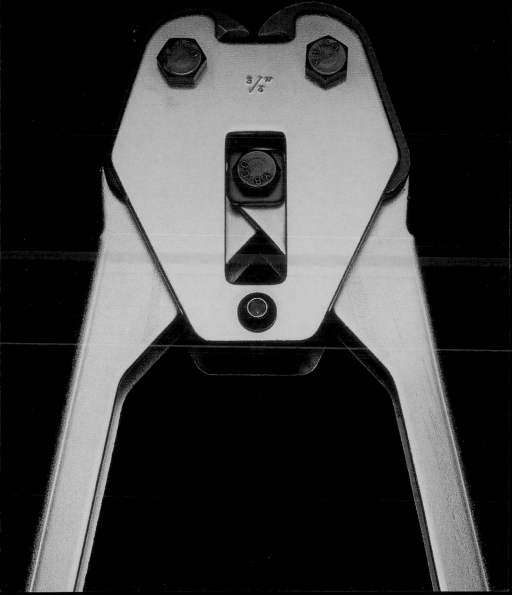

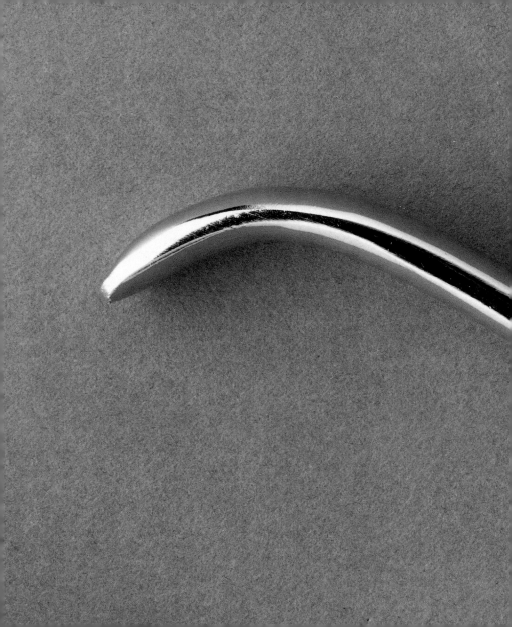

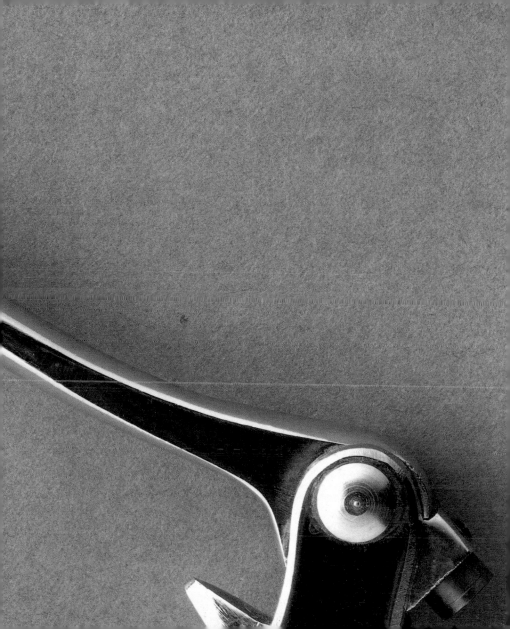

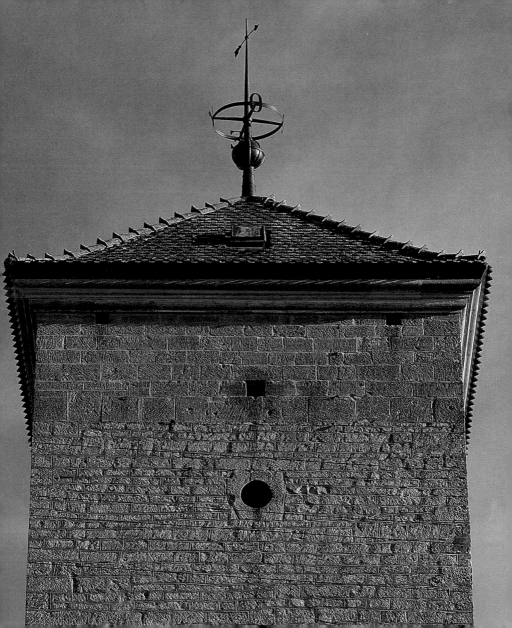

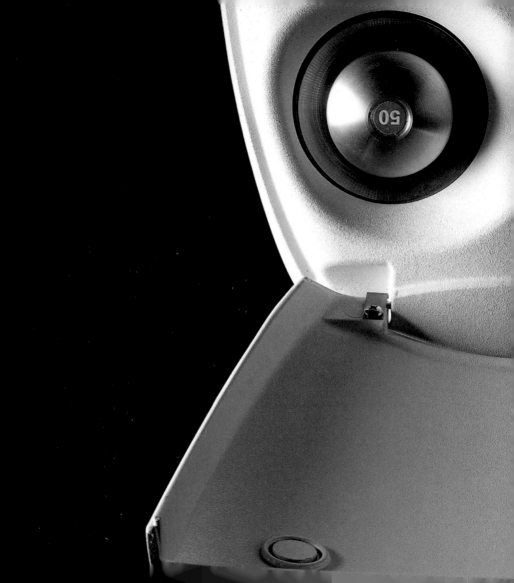

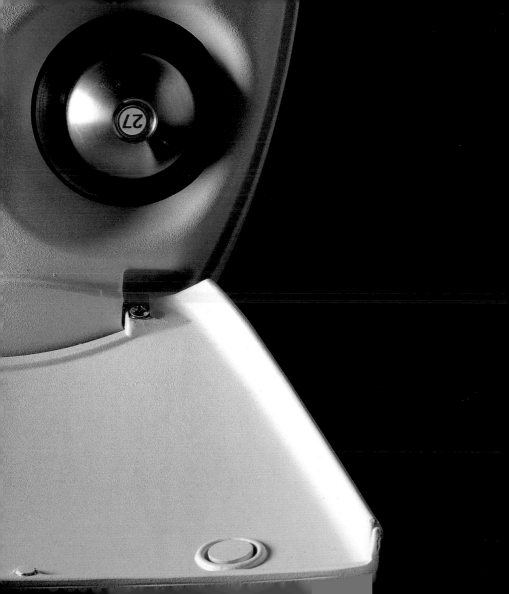

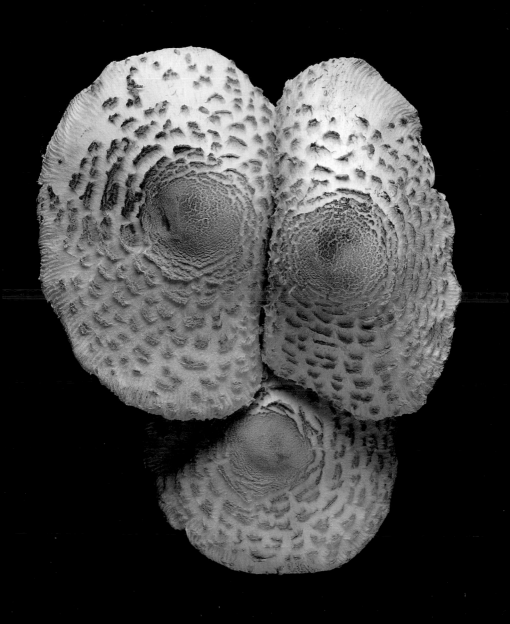

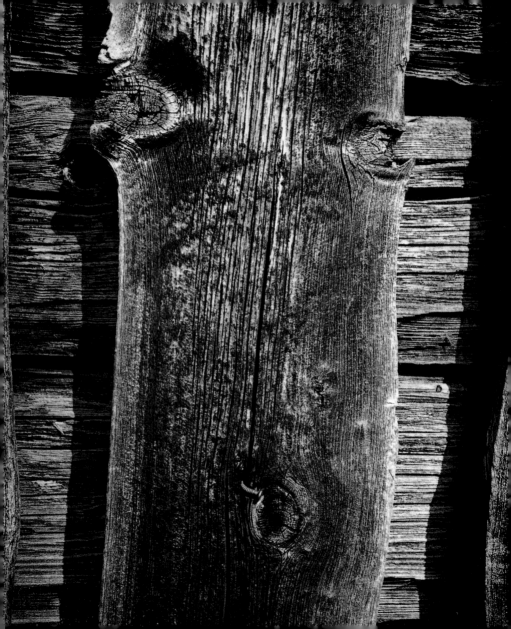

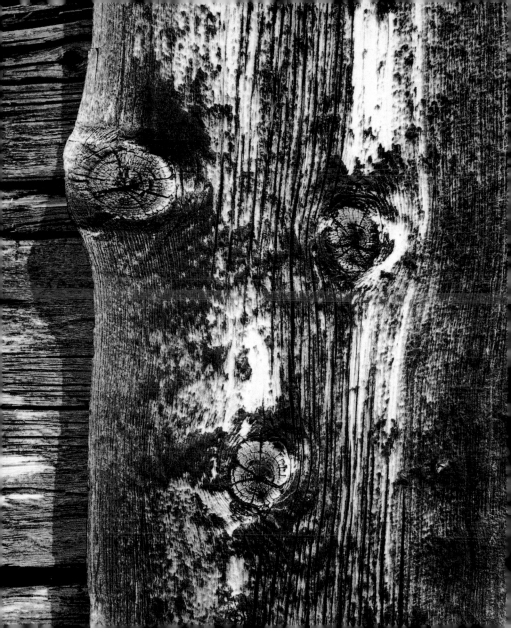

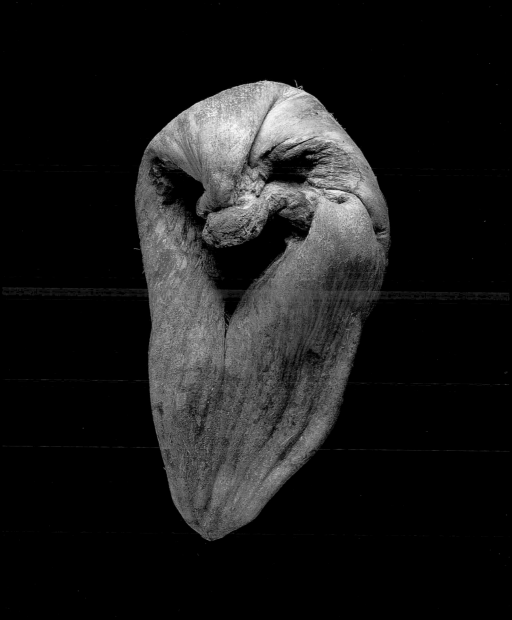

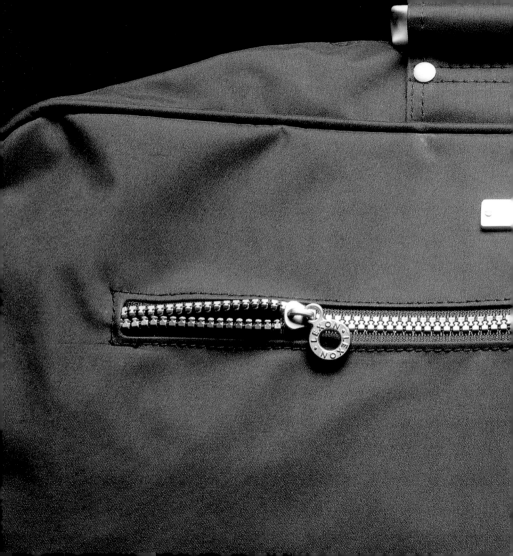

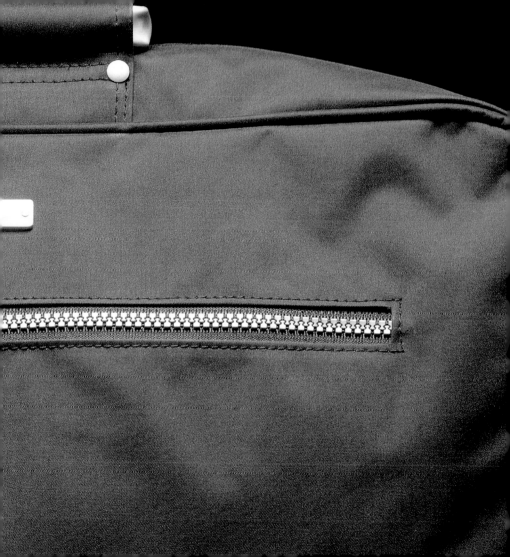

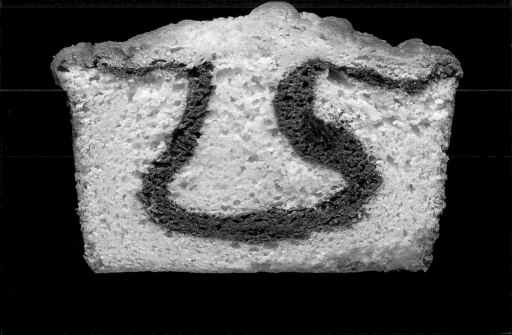

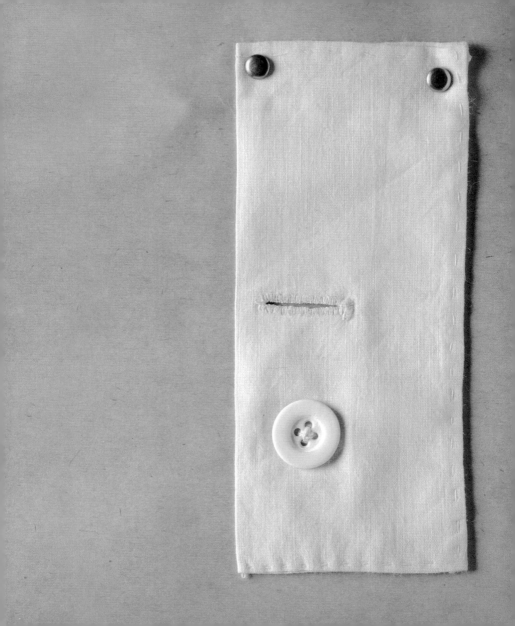

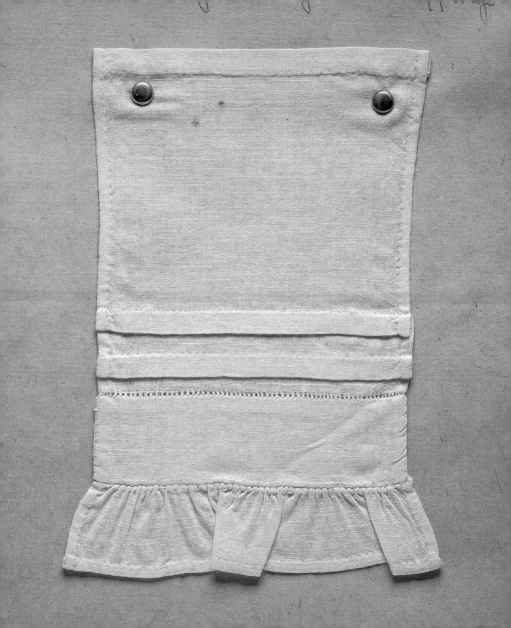

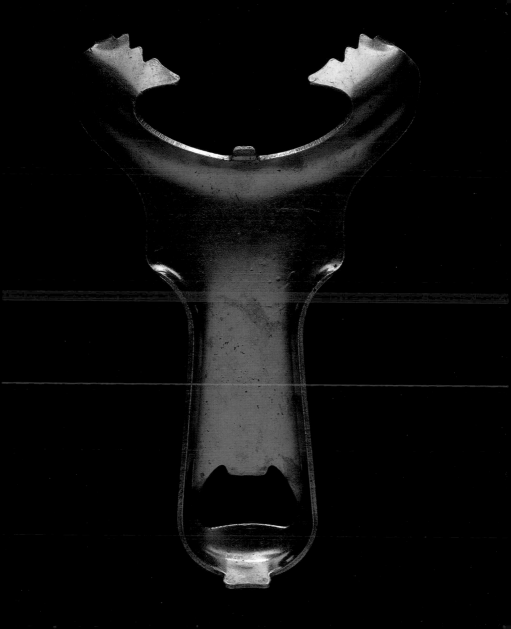

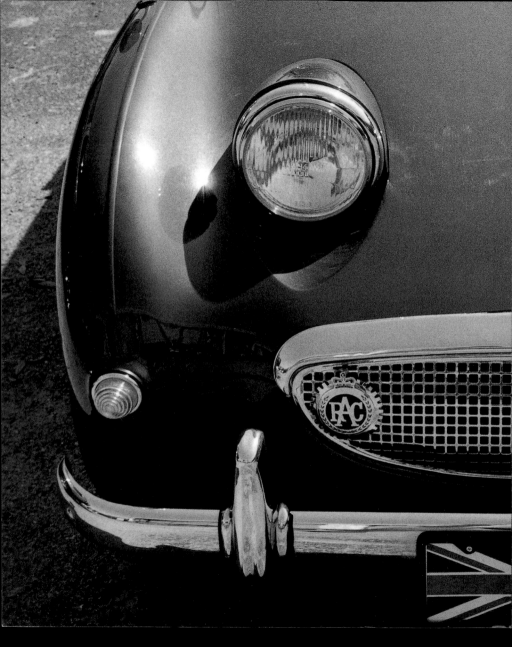

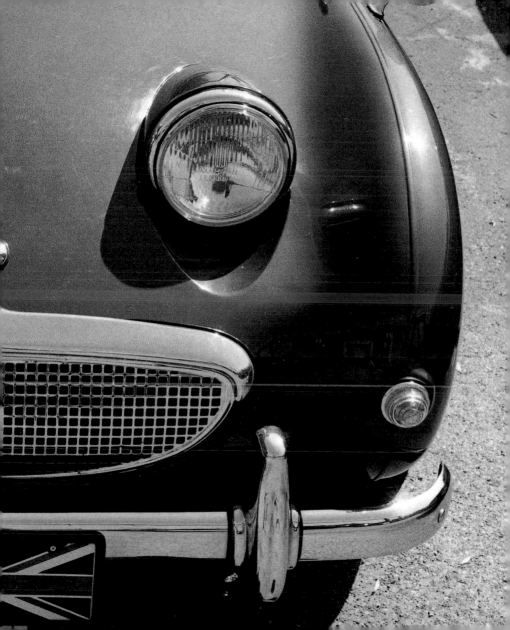

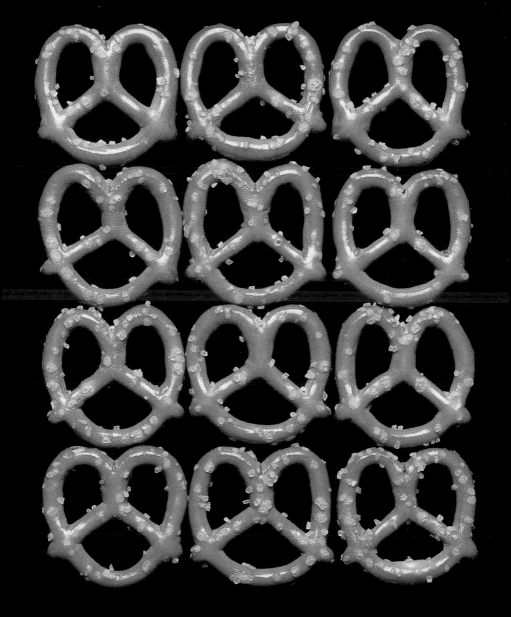

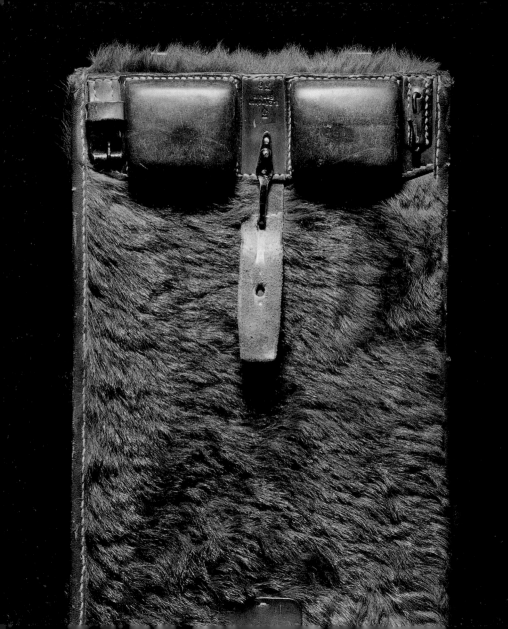

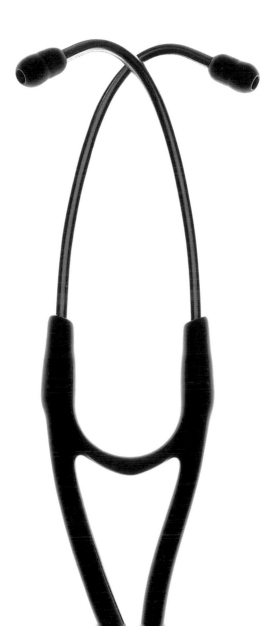

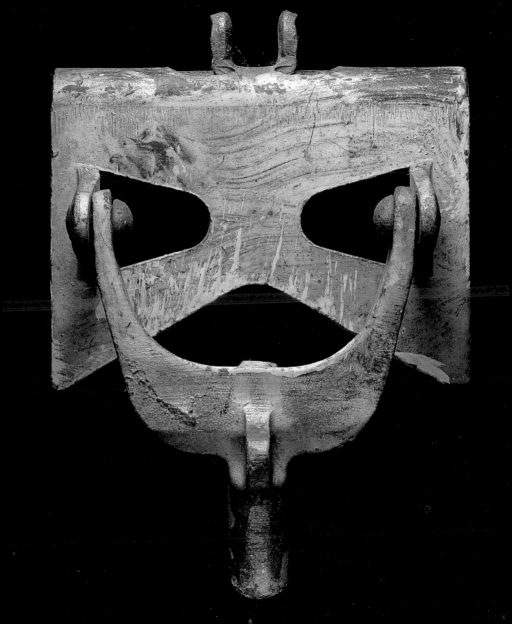

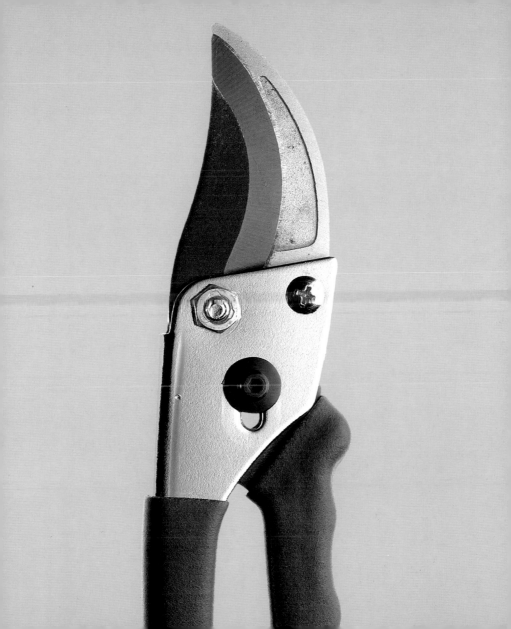

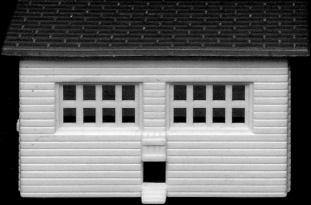

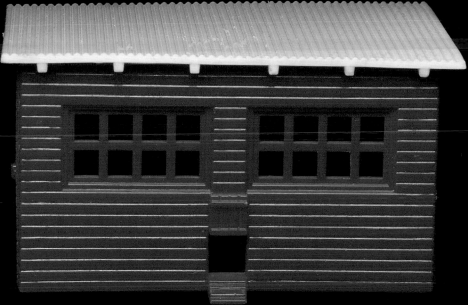

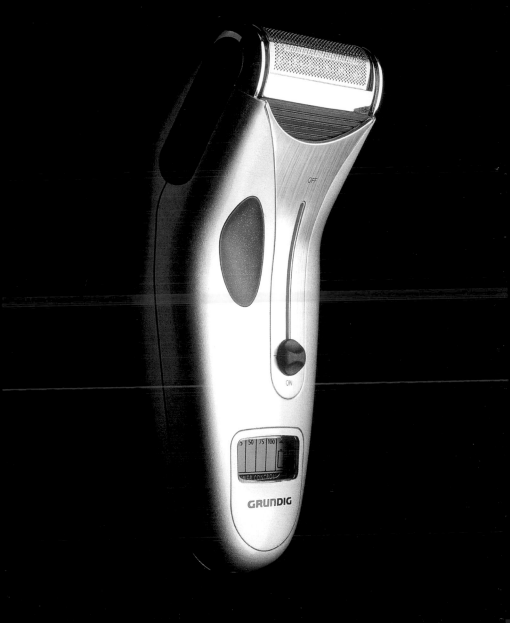

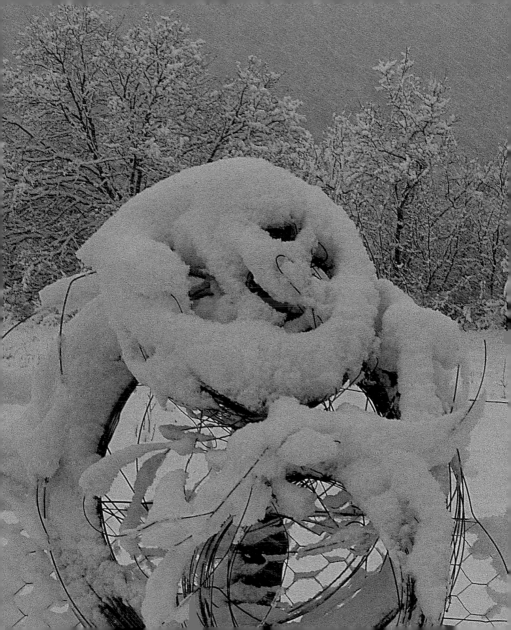

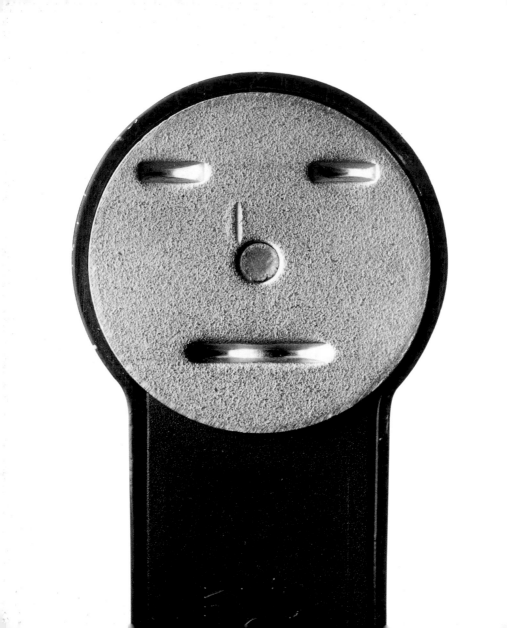

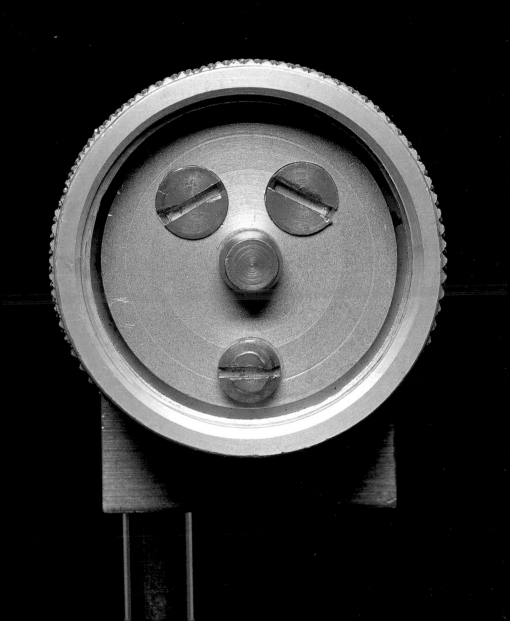

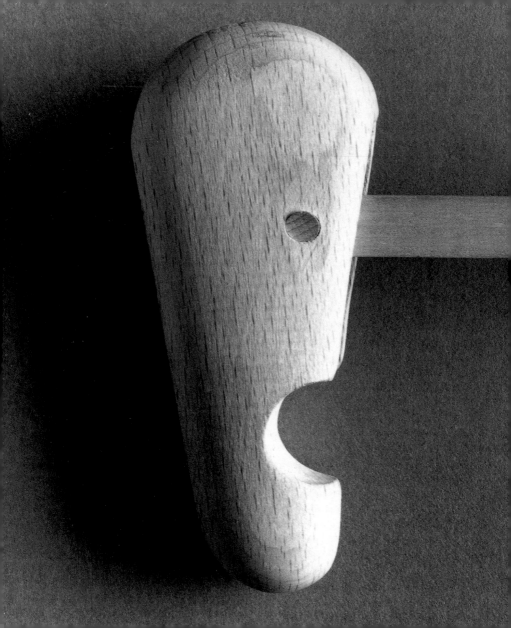

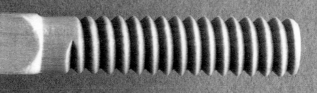

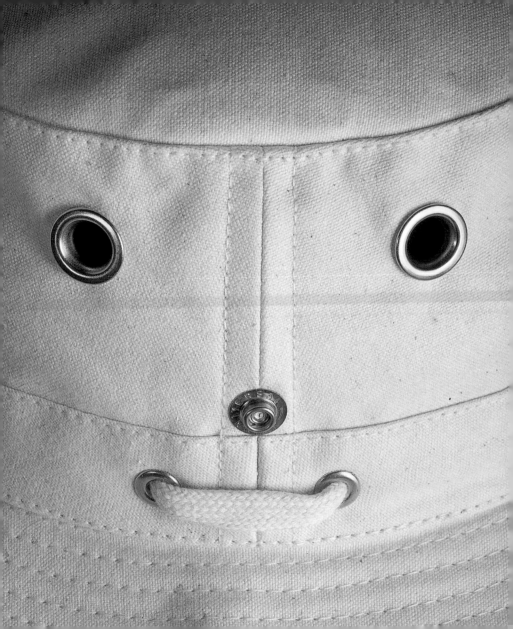

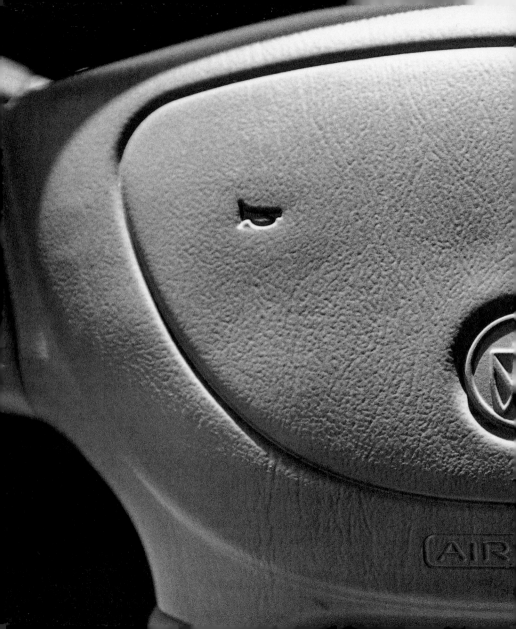

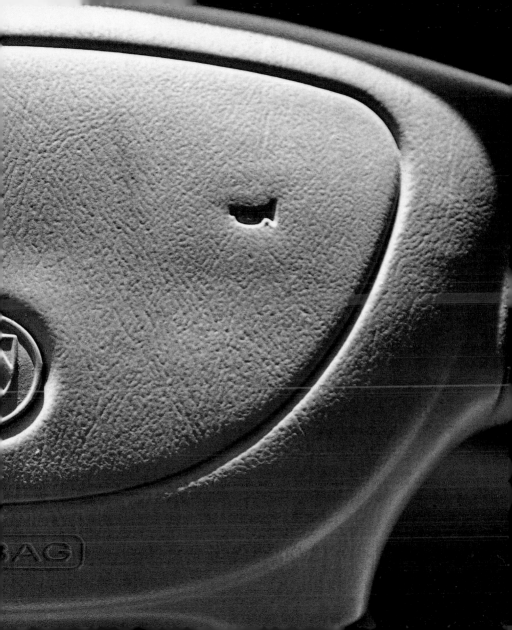

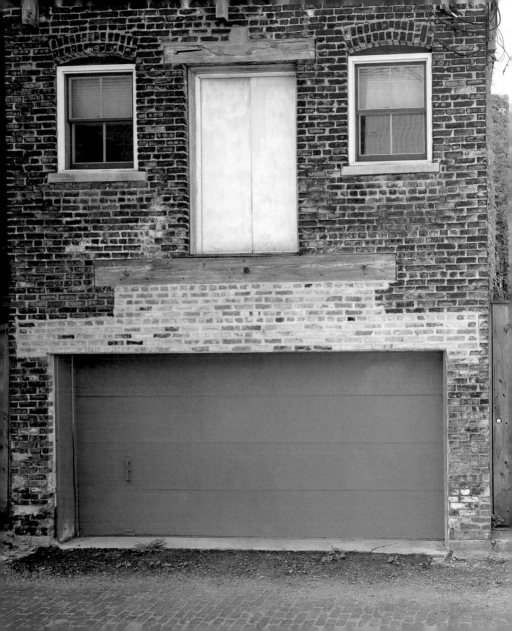

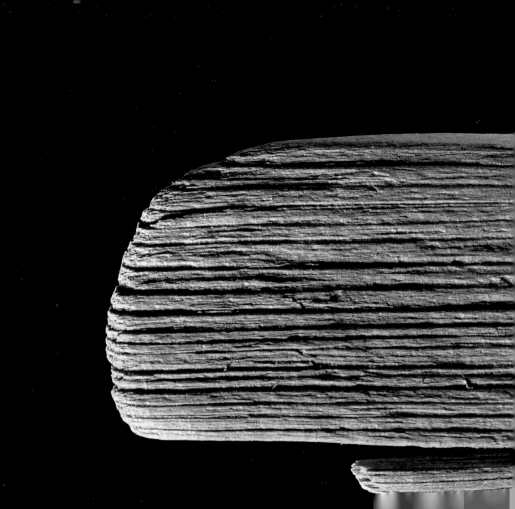

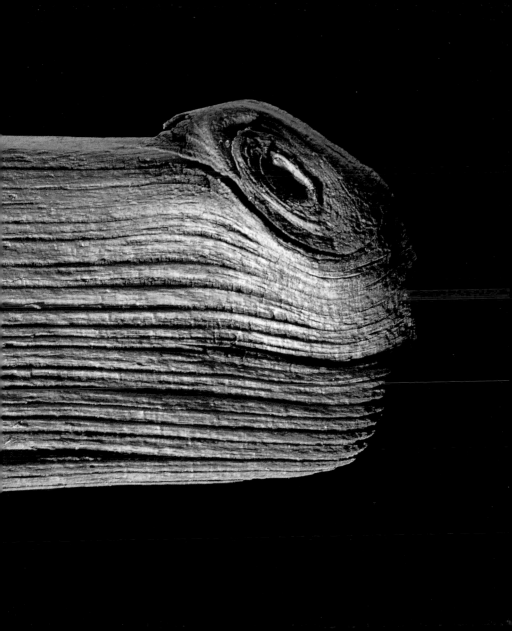

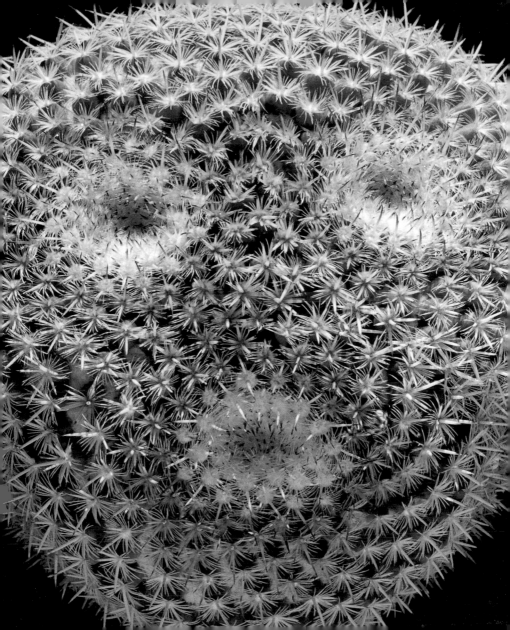

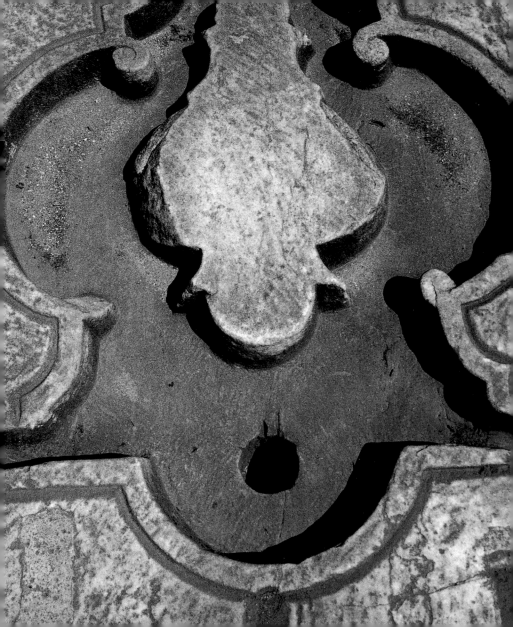

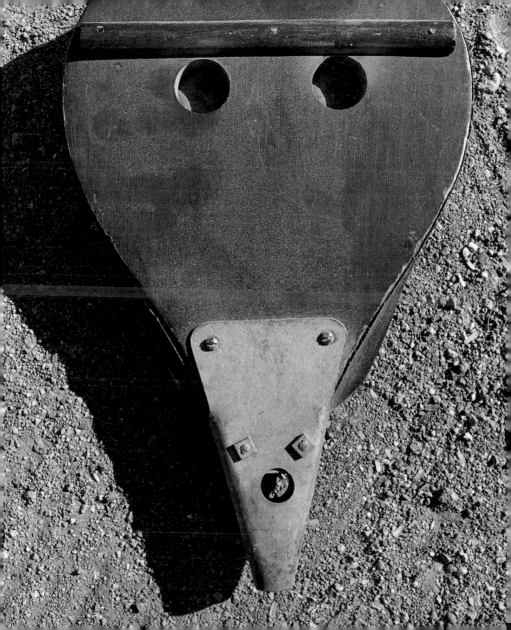

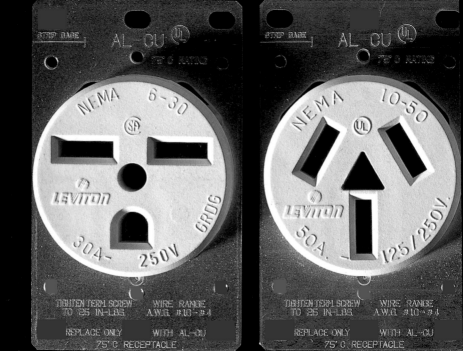

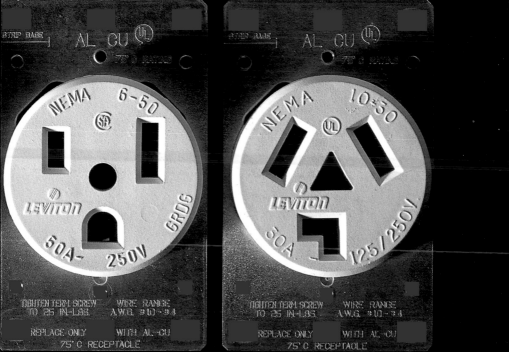

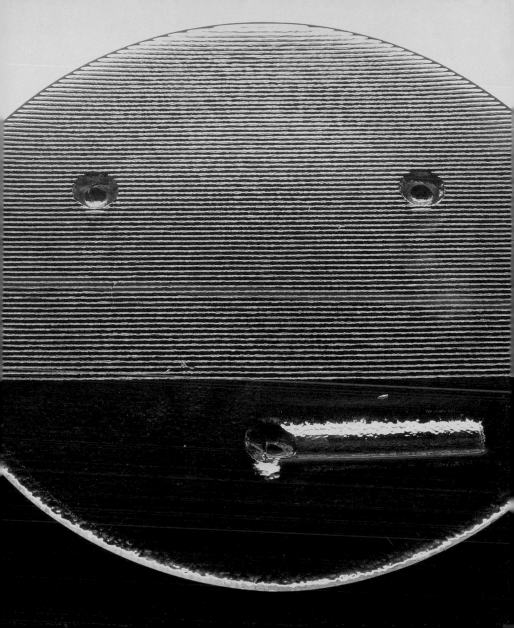

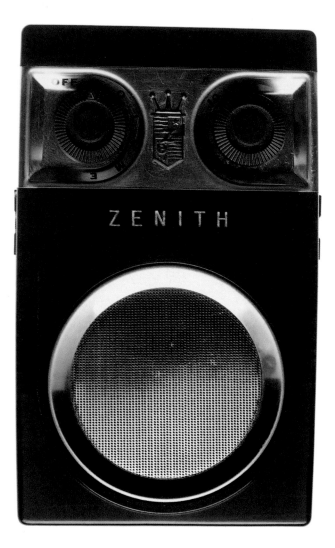

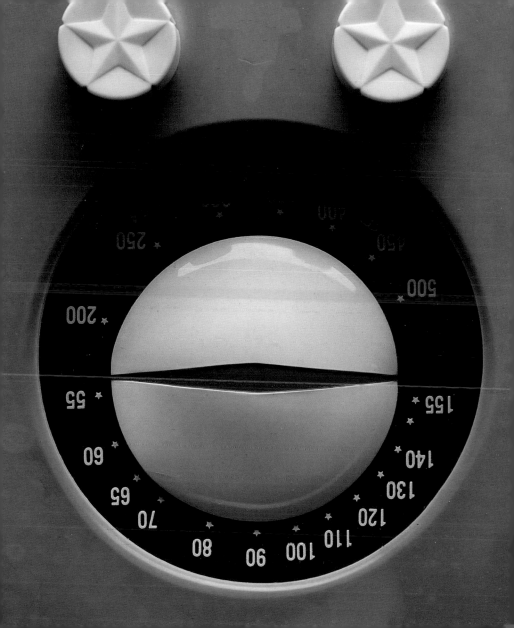

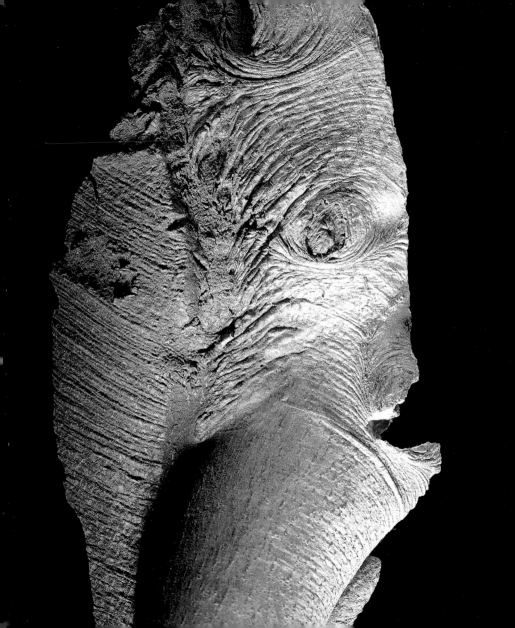

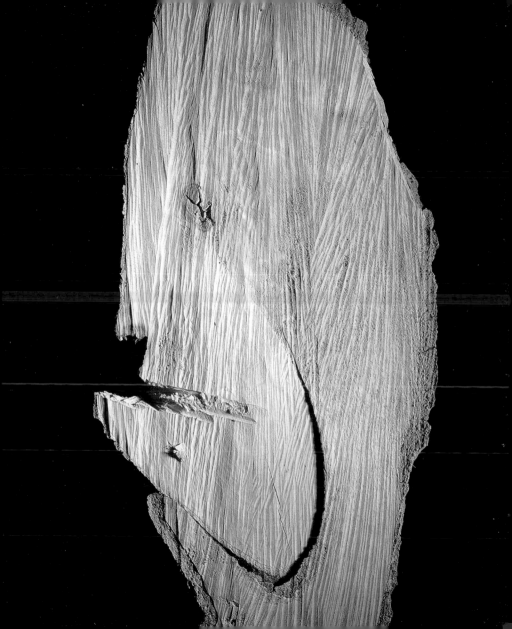

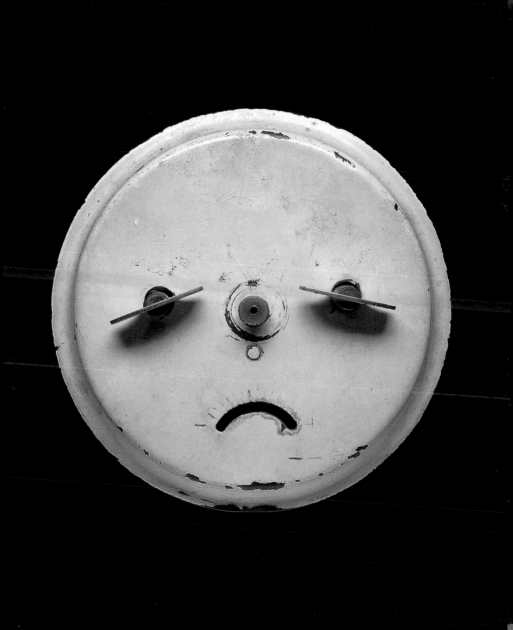

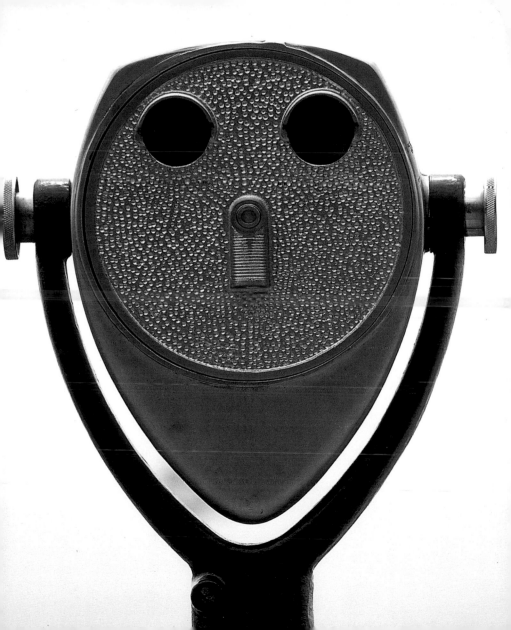